P9-EDI-183

best sex writing
2013

HILLSBORO PUBLIC LIBRARY
Hillsboro, OR
WITHDRAWN
Member of Washington County
COOPERATIVE LIBRARY SERVICES

best sex writing
2013
The State of Today's Sexual Culture

Edited by
Rachel Kramer Bussel

Guest Judge
Carol Queen, PhD

CLEiS
PRESS

Copyright © 2013 by Rachel Kramer Bussel.
Foreword copyright © 2013 by Carol Queen.

All rights reserved. Except for brief passages quoted in newspaper, magazine, radio, television, or online reviews, no part of this book may be reproduced in any form or by any means, electronic or mechanical, including photocopying or recording, or by information storage or retrieval system, without permission in writing from the publisher.

Published in the United States by Cleis Press, Inc., 2246 Sixth Street, Berkeley, California 94710.

Printed in the United States.
Cover design: Scott Idleman/Blink
Cover photograph: Thinkstock Images
Text design: Frank Wiedemann

First Edition.
10 9 8 7 6 5 4 3 2 1

Trade paper ISBN: 978-1-57344-899-4
E-book ISBN: 978-1-57344-916-8

Permissions acknowledgments for the essays reprinted in this book may be found on page 229.

Library of Congress Cataloging-in-Publication Data

Best sex writing 2013 / edited by Rachel Kramer Bussel.
    pages cm
Includes bibliographical references and index.
ISBN 978-1-57344-899-4 (pbk. : alk. paper)
1. Sex--United States. I. Bussel, Rachel Kramer.

HQ18.U5B45 2013
306.70973--dc23

                                        2013002069

5115 3053
4/13

CONTENTS

Foreword
Carol Queen, PhD

If you need any indication beyond that provided by particle physics that we occupy a world containing more than one dimension, look no further than contemporary Western discourse on sex. In the United States, especially, the time/space continuum points toward a diverse future—how are sexual cultures developing and transitioning into twenty-first-century entities? How is a changed, expanded landscape of sexual communities and erotic choices, facilitated by the gods of the Internet, altering the path of growing up, finding oneself, decoding all our culture's mysterious sex signals, meeting and mating and doing it some more? Plenty of contributors in *Best Sex Writing 2013* shed light, or at least drop crumbs, to help as we consider this.

And yet! On the other hand, the Scarecrow's arms are crossed and he simultaneously points forward and back. This way! That way! And people who have been influenced by way-post-sexual-revolution, feminist, and sex-positive ideas now watch with amazement as linear time morphs, shimmers and wiggles like the suddenly-visible air above a blacktop road on a hot summer day, and serious political discourse includes ideas about gender roles, contraception, homosexuality, abortion, and censorship that made me, at least, wonder whether Anthony Comstock might return from the dead to join the Republican presidential ticket. Paul Ryan: a reanimate?

I'm associated with sex education, pleasure activism, erotic diversity and sex-positivity; there have been loads of interesting progress on all these fronts over the past couple of decades, as the many ways one can experience or desire sex and relationship have shattered, scintillating into a spectrum of identities and communities. All of these, except maybe Furries, have always been part of the private, even secret, landscape of erotic drive, choice, or chance: our great-great grandmas had vibrators, artists documented their own and their lovers' erotic bodies in the 1920s (and certainly before), Samuel Steward let Alfred Kinsey set him up with an SM dominant in 1952, and Virginia Woolf had more than one partner and wrote a gender-bending novel about one of them. There's next to nothing new under the sun, sex-wise—but now pretty much all these identities, the ways we learn about possibility and are affirmed in our desires (or at least find porn that reflects it or partners willing to engage in it), have stepped into the light of day, into Google searches and Facebook groups.

At the same time, it's yesterday once more. Haters hate, bullies bully, and young people kill themselves because they can't believe a future full of love and pleasure waits for them. That's really no surprise; it's way easier to fill a conference hall with thousands of kinky people than it is to get a public school to represent sexuality as something other than a danger, especially sexuality that is non-heteronormative. Actually, too many young people get no message at all that alternative sexualities exist *and* that they might have something to do with them. And you can be as heteronormative as you please and get out of high school not understanding anything about the clitoris.

A society fixated on and yet fearful about sex exists today as surely as it did in my mother's time, and then as now it enables sexual abuse, erotic cluelessness, us-and-them belief systems. If anything, the latter is worse now than it was in the longer-ago past, because my mom and dad weren't even sure, in the 1940s, what a homosexual was—now, alongside all the amazing gains that have been made, this culture is polarized over sexuality from stem to stern.

But that's not the half of it. Here in the twenty-first century, land of progress, my specialized Google News search (set to "sexuality"—isn't yours?) brings me mostly LGBT results. Is it so little understood that *everyone* has a sexuality? That it can be as diverse with varying desires among heteros as among queers? That sexual *orientation* is not, in fact, the definition of sexuality; that knowing someone's sexual orientation does not give you a true idea of that person's sexuality, their *sexual* preferences, only really revealing the gender/s of the person/s with whom they'd like to engage in that sex? Gay, straight and everybody else: any of us can be vanilla or kinky, monogamous or polyamorous or open, fetishistic (in a thousand different ways), into the person and not the gender, into no one but gender variants, even asexual and into no one at all. (At least, not *that way*.) We can have safer sex or bareback; we can feel more erotically alive in a costume than we do out of it; we can charge money or fuck for free; we can be shy or brazen, exhibitionistic or private, only in it for love or only in it for the orgasm. And of course we can be many of these things at once, or morph fluidly (or very bumpily) from one identity or set of desires to another.

Really, there are more than seven billion sexual orientations. If the turn-back-the-clockers understood how really, truly diverse sexuality is, some of their heads would explode, and maybe the rest would leave their target populations alone and stow the opprobrium—about sex, at least. It makes a bigger sexual world for them, too, of course, not just those of us already identified as Other. The irony of this vast rend in the cultural fabric is the way more information feeds both sides: fear and loathing or excitement and relief, we have in common this range of reactions to a very big and sexy cat who has well and truly escaped its bag.

We can't do justice to all of this in one volume, but we can pack *Best Sex Writing 2013* with the best essays and journalism we can find, reminding you how much variety, difference and drama can be found when we till the ground of desire. I hope this inspires you to take your own sexual reality seriously, and to consider in what ways you're unique—and how surprisingly well you may relate to the stories of those very different from yourself. It's the only way we'll bridge this gap, heal the rift in the space/time continuum of sex: really listening to the stories we all have to tell.

Introduction:
A Different Kind of Sexual Education

As editor of the *Best Sex Writing* series, and a writer about sex in both fiction and nonfiction forms, I'm privileged to hear from lots of people about sexuality, whether asking for advice or wanting to talk about the big issues of the day, whether that means attacks on birth control or *Fifty Shades of Grey*. The biggest thing I've learned, though, is pretty basic: we are all always learning. You can indeed get a PhD in sexology, like foreword author and contributor Carol Queen did, but that doesn't mean you simply give up and assume you know everything about the wide world of sexuality and sexual variation. You can't; it's impossible.

Part of why sex writing is so vital is because we all have things to learn—about ourselves, and about others. While this book will not teach you how to have sex, you will learn about what motivates others in their sexual desires, whether to engage in multiple relationships, perform sex work, come out as bisexual, build increasingly advanced vibrators, or more.

I think it's safe to say that whether this is the first book about sex you've ever read or the thousandth, you will learn something about what makes people tick, about sexual desire and sexual community. The latter is as important to me as the former, because it's within the community of sex writers, educators and activists that I've carved out a place for myself as a bisexual, feminist, kinky sex writer. Lori Selke writes in her open letter, "Dear John," about feeling disillusioned by the judgments being passed around her local leather community: "See, my kinky leather identity grew firmly out of my queerness and my feminism. All three of those elements are important and in some ways inseparable. It's important to me to pursue the sort of social justice that ensures that our consensual relationships are someday entered into from a place of roughly equal societal power. Without that aim, we're simply perpetuating oppression." I suspect many people aren't aware of just how committed to their ideals those in the kink and leather communities are. To assume it's all about whips, chains, bondage and spanking is to miss the point—of course it's about those things, but it's also about much more.

The educational lessons here are often much more personal. When Conner Habib opens his essay "Rest Stop Confidential" with, "I was fifteen the first time I found out that men have sex in public," I must admit that, at thirty-seven, I have only seen men having sex in public at parties specifically designed for sex. The first of many firsts Julia Serano details in "Cherry Picking" begins, "The first time I learned about sex was in fifth grade." We are all both capable of learning more, and impacted by what we did—or didn't—learn about sex at a young age.

Some of what you're about to read is sad or scary or disheartening; I cannot promise you a book of shiny happy sex bouncing off every page, because that is not the world we live in. There are laws to fight against, AIDS plaguing the gay community, internalized oppression, questions that may have no answers, or multiple answers. I didn't select these essays and articles because they purport to have all the answers.

Last year's guest judge, the noted sexual commentator Susie Bright, when asked about *The Guardian's* Bad Sex award, responded, "There is no art without sex." I think the same could be said for the news; sex is not a topic squirreled away on the back page of the paper; it's on the front page, in the sports section, the business section, the editorials. It's covered in fashion magazines and newsweeklies. In *Best Sex Writing 2013*, hot topics include New York Jets quarterback Tim Tebow's virginity and the laws governing condom use in porn.

Sex education remains at the forefront of the news and continues to be "controversial," though, like birth control, another political battleground of late in the United States, I would think it would be a no-brainer. Yet I can still read articles like one in *Time*[1] about the Mississippi county, Tunica, with the highest teen pregnancy rate that is only recently getting on board with sex ed, via a law mandating it do so: "During the four years Ashley McKay attended Rosa Fort High School in Tunica, Miss., her sex education consisted mainly of an instructor listing different sexually transmitted diseases. 'There was no curriculum,' she says. 'The teacher, an older gentleman who was also the football coach, would tell us, *If you get AIDS, you're gonna die. Pick out your casket, because you're gonna die.*'"

We should not be reading articles like this any longer, but we are, and it's not just youths who are in dire need of sex

---

1   http://nation.time.com/2012/09/21/sex-education-in-mississippi-will-a-new-law-lower-teen-pregnancy-rates/

education. Just today, I received an email from an acquaintance asking if I could chat because, "I have found a wonderful woman with whom I have begun to explore areas of my sexuality I really have never followed through on or even verbally fantasized about." He has questions. So do many people, but they don't know where to turn.

This book doesn't purport to have all the answers, and is likely to raise many discussions and propose multiple answers to questions about open relationships, prostitution, sexual orientation and other topics. It cannot take the place of talking about sex—with your lovers, friends, parents, children, neighbors and coworkers. Those shouldn't be the same conversations, but they can exist, and by making sex a topic we don't shy away from, we start to educate ourselves about what others are thinking, feeling and doing. So I hope that you won't read this book and keep it tucked away on your bookshelf (or e-reader); while you are more than welcome to do so, I hope you will introduce some part of what you've read into a conversation, take it off the page and into real life. You will very likely learn something, and that is a process that can easily snowball; there's never an end, because it's a lifelong process, one that I look forward to every day.

Rachel Kramer Bussel
New York City

Live Nude Models
Jonathan Lethem

Be careful what you wish for; you may turn out to have already
had it. That's to say, to have had it before you could make intelli-
gible use of it, perhaps before you could get your synapses to parse
it for what it was. By the time I was seventeen years old and had a
girlfriend who would take her clothes off (there had been one at
fifteen who, serially, entrancingly, wouldn't), I'd been envision-
ing women with their clothes off, ravishing them with the secret
lidless eyeball of my brain, for at least five years. Though these
were five long, aching years, which I took entirely personally at
the time, I do realize how mundane such a confession must be. Is.
There wasn't anything baroque or complicated in my pining visu-
alizations or the procedure by which I took their edge off, and it's
surely the case that a savvy person glancing my way would guess
I did pretty well nothing else of note at the time.

Here's what's un-mundane: in that same span, through my

rude, ripened, teen-prime years, there were live nude models appearing nightly in my home—women to whose unclad forms my ordinary, lidded eyeballs had regular access. My father painted them, upstairs in his studio. "Nightly" may exaggerate, but through those years nudes were the main subject of his large oils on canvas, of which he painted dozens—sometimes from memory or from studies but often with the body present before him—as well as generating many hundreds of nudes on paper or vinyl, in pencil, oil crayons or gouache or combinations of those mediums, nearly each and every one of which was done in the presence of what at eight or ten I would have still called "a naked lady" (or, rarely, but it bears mentioning, in the presence of a naked man).

Me, I opened the door. I walked through. My father's studio was part of our home. I did this, probably, beginning at twelve or thirteen, when I would have learned to refer to the naked ladies in question as "models," as in a mock-casual formulation like, "We can hang out in the kitchen, my dad's up with one of his models," or the defensively sophisticated, "Sure, I see the models with their clothes off, it's no big deal." I do recall forming sentences like these, just as I recall the slightly widened eyes of the models themselves, a few times, as they met the eyes of the would-be jaded twelve-year-old who'd pushed through the door without knocking. I can also bring up a good portion of ambience (visual aspects of which are confirmed by the paintings themselves): the musty throw rugs and scarred chairs and hand-carpentered easels and exposed-brick wall; the upright, soldered-iron wood-burning stove my father later installed; the jazz or blues or (less often) leftist news and culture-gab of WBAI seeping from the cassette-playing boom box; the savor of brushes marinating in turpentine and tangy odor of the cake of Lava soap—the only brand, my father explained, that would gently strip oil paint from human

skin—at the shallow porcelain sink; the bulletin board layered
with valentines from my mother and enigmatic newspaper clip-
pings (the death of Karl Wallenda was one) that would inspire
later work of my father's, et cetera. What I can't supply, despite
the clamor I by now imagine I hear from my reader on this point,
is an account of any parent-child consultations on the topic of the
models and how I was or wasn't supposed to feel about them. I
can't supply these because, I'm fairly certain, they didn't occur.
Nudity Is Fine, like Nixon Is a Vampire or Grown-Ups Smoke
Pot, was a truth floating in our house, the sort I gradually inferred
was somewhat more true inside our doors than out.

I not only glimpsed the models. At twelve or thirteen I de-
clared myself an apprentice artist and began to draw them myself.
Not in the studio upstairs, or rarely there. Mostly I went along
with my dad on "drawing group" night, to the home of his artist
friends Bob and Cynthia, a loft space on Atlantic Avenue with
square footage enough for a model to stand encircled by seven
or eight artists sitting with sketch pads braced on crossed legs, or
seated before small easels. Specifically, seven adult artists (though
my father was their elder statesman, likely at least a decade older
than any of the others) and one teenager. Young teenager. I began
before high school—I know this for certain because there were
nudes in the portfolio of sketches I used to win entry into the
High School of Music and Art that year. I was a regular at drawing group for three years, I'd guess. By the time I was sixteen I
was through hanging out with my dad, for a while at least. But
for three years I soaked my eyeballs in live flesh—not even a kid
who'd grown up at a nudist colony could have been invited to
stare like I stared. After all, I was an artist.

No one balked at my presence. This was 1977, 1978. The
models, so far as I can rely on these memory tendrils I'm chasing,

were blasé. These were mostly art students themselves, settled into an easy if boring gig. Likely posing for a group of men and women together was more comfortable, generally, than making a private exhibition for a solitary male, and evenings at Bob and Cynthia's were convivial. The routine followed the lines of every life-drawing class since publication of Kimon Nicolaides's *The Natural Way to Draw* and probably long before it: a series of rapid-fire poses so the artists could loosen with gestural sketches, then five- or ten-minute poses, then a few held long enough for a study—also long enough that the model might pause to stretch or even don a robe and take a five-minute break before resuming. Between poses the artists wandered to see others' work, and I did this too. Sometimes the models roamed too, in their robes. Other times they were uninterested in the results. I worked with Cray-Pas or gray or colored pencil, or compressed charcoal and, less often, painted in watercolor and gouache. I was less patient than the adults—I was there learning patience, as much as any-thing—and remember feeling "finished" with studies before the longer poses were done and then watching the clock. Apart from that lapse I worked in absorption, as with all absorbing work since I recall precisely zero from the mental interior of the experience.

What I wasn't doing—I'd know—was mental slavering. The Tex Avery wolf of sexual voraciousness not only restrained his eyeballs from first swelling like dirigibles and then bursting like loaded cigars, he slept. Any account of the evolutionary "hard-wiring" of lust is stuck, I guess, dismissing me now as an outlier, or just a liar. The superextensive actuality of women's bodies be-fore my eyes was either too much or too little for me to make masturbatory mincemeat of. Both too much and too little: the scrutiny was too much, the context too little. I don't mean they weren't sexy bodies. I'd guess they were. But Jonathan-seeing-them wasn't sexy at all. Even as I recorded with my charcoal or crayon the halo of untrimmed pubic bush and the flesh-braid of mystery that it haloed, I attained a total non-purchase on those bodies as objects of desire. The palace of lust was a site under construction—that's what I was off doing at night or afternoons, fantasizing about girls I knew who'd never even show me their knees. Then I slavered plenty.

Did I, in my imaginings, substitute for my non-girlfriends' un-conquerable forms the visual stuff I'd gleaned at drawing group? Nope. As much as a T-shirt's neckline or tube top's horizon might seem a cruel limit to my wondering gaze, I didn't want my imagination to supply the pink pebbly fact of aureole and nipple like those I'd examined under bright light for hours at a time. It wasn't that I found real women's bodies unappetizing but that I didn't have any use for them in the absolute visual sphere within which I'd gained access. Much like a person who's disappointed or confused at seeing the face attached to the voice of a radio personality well known to their ears and then realizes that no face would have seemed any more appropriate, I suspect I didn't really make mental nudie shots of girls my age. I didn't picture them undressed; I imagined undressing them and the situations in which such a thing would be imaginable. My eyeballs wanted to be fingertips. I was a romantic.

A romantic teenage boy, that is. My romance encompassed a craving for illicit glimpses, not because I lacked visual informa-tion but as rehearsals of transgression and discovery. A craving for craving, especially in the social context of other teenage boys, that mass of horny romantics. But we're talking about a terrible low point in the history of teenage access to pornography: Ev-eryone's dad had canceled his *Playboy* subscription in a simulta-neous feminist epiphany a few years before (that everyone's dad had once subscribed to *Playboy* was a golden myth; I trust it was halfway true). The Internet was a millennium away. A friend and I were actually excited when we discovered a cache of back issues of *Sexology,* a black-and-white crypto-scientific pulp magazine, in the plaster and lathe of a ruined brownstone on Wyckoff Street. Pity us. When a couple of snootily gorgeous older teenage girls suddenly moved into the upper duplex of a house on Dean Street, there was some talk among the block's boys about climbing a nearby tree for a leer, a notion as halcyon-suburban as anything in my childhood. But the London plane trees shading our block had no branches low enough to be climbable, had likely been selected precisely for their resistance to burglars. The point is, I was as thrilled to imagine glimpsing the sisters as any of the other schemers. I could very well have gone off to drawing group the evening of that same day but made no mental conjugation between the desired object and the wasted abundance before me.

Only two uneasy memories bridge this gulf, between the eunuch-child who breezed through a world of live nude models and the hormonal disaster site I was the rest of the time. One glitch was the constant threat or promise that a drawing group model would cancel at the last minute, since tradition had it that one of the circle would volunteer for duty instead. Two of the group's members were younger women—named, incredibly enough, Hazel and Laurel—for whom I harbored modest but definite boy-to-woman crushes and with whom I may have managed even to be legibly flirtatious. If one evening a model had canceled and either Hazel or Laurel took her clothes off, I'd likely have been pitched headfirst into the chasm of my disassociation. I never faced this outcome. The only substitute model ever to volunteer on my watch was our host, the hairily cherubic Bobby Ramirez. But I would never forget what *didn't* happen, who *didn't* undress.

You may choose to see this as evidence against my assertion that the scene was not a sexual one for me. I choose to see it as certifying proof of my capacity for fantasizing about clothed women who lingered in the periphery of my vision *at the exact instant* I ignored naked ones in the center of my vision.

The second slippage took place not at drawing group but in my room, with my friend Karl. We were fourteen. Karl and I usually drew superhero comics together, but this afternoon, deep into the porn drought of the 1970s, we drifted into trying to produce our own, doodling fantasy females without the veil of a cape or utility belt. At one point Karl reached an impasse in his attempt to do justice to the naked lady in his mind's eye and let me analyze the problem. Yes, the nipples were too small, and placed too high, on the gargantuan breasts Karl had conjured. He'd also too much defaulted to the slim, squared-off frame of the supermen we'd been compulsively perfecting. "Do you mind?" I asked. Taking the drawing from Karl, I compacted and softened the torso and widened the hips, gave his fantasy volume and weight, splitting the difference between the unreal ratio and something more persuasive. He'd handed me a teenage boy's fantasy and I, a teenage boy, passed back a woman, even if one who'd need back surgery in the long run. Karl and I were both, I think, unnerved, and we never returned to this exact pursuit. Our next crack at DIY porn was retrograde and bawdy, a comic called *Super-Dick,* with images that were barely better than stick figures.

Confessing for the first time my authorship of *Super-Dick,* I'm flabbergasted, not at the dereliction of parental authority that would traipse nude women past the gaze of a boy still excited to sketch with ballpoint pen a hieroglyphic cock-and-balls in cape and boots and have it catapult into the obliging hairy face of a villain named Pussy-Man, but at the Möbius strip of consciousness that enabled that boy to walk around believing himself a single person instead of two or a hundred. If I've bet my life's work on a suspicion that we live at least as much in our wishes and dreams, our constructions and projections, as we do in any real waking life, the existence of which we can demonstrate by rapping it with our knuckles, perhaps my non-utilization of the live nude models helped me place the bet. How could I ever be astonished to see how we human animals slide into the vicarious at the faintest invitation, leaving vast flaming puddings of the Real uneaten? I did.

My last year at the High School of Music and Art a teacher booked a nude model for us to draw in an advanced drawing class, one consisting only of graduating seniors. By chance this was the last time I'd ever sketch from a nude model, though I couldn't have known it at the time. By implication this was a privilege we seniors had earned after four years of art school: to be treated like adults. Still, there was plenty of nervous joking in the days before, and, when the moment came, the doors and windows were kept carefully shaded against eyes other than those of us in the class. Needless to say, I felt blasé for several reasons, not least my own recent sexual initiation. I'd also begun to reformat myself as a future writer rather than an apprentice artist (at seventeen I'd already been an apprentice artist a long time), and everything to do with my final high school semester felt beneath my serious attention.

Yet ironically, I'll never forget the model that day. I remember her body when I've forgotten the others—had forgotten them, usually, by the time I'd begun spraying fixative on my last drawing of them, before they'd finished dressing. I remember her not because she was either uncannily gorgeous or ugly, or because I experienced some disconcerting arousal, but for an eye-grabbing anatomical feature: the most protuberant clitoris I'd seen, or have since. This wasn't something I could have found language to explain to my fellow students that day, if I wanted to (I didn't). The model showed no discomfort with her body. She posed, beneath vile fluorescence, standing atop the wobbling, standard-issue New York City Department of Education tables I'd been around my whole life, the four legs of which never seemed capable of reaching the floor simultaneously, and we thirty-odd teenagers drew her, the whole of us sober, respectfully hushed, a trace bored if you were me, but anyhow living up to the teacher's expectation. But I do remember thinking: *I know and they don't.* (The boys, that would be who I meant.) I remember thinking: *They'll think they're all that way.*

Can a Better Vibrator Inspire an Age of Great American Sex?

Andy Isaacson

The offices of Jimmyjane are above a boarded-up dive bar in San Francisco's Mission district. There used to be a sign on a now-unmarked side door, until employees grew weary of men showing up in a panic on Valentine's Day thinking they could buy last-minute gifts there. (They can't.) The only legacy that remains of the space's original occupant, an underground lesbian club, is a large fireplace set into the back wall. Porcelain massage candles and ceramic stones, neatly displayed on sleek white shelves alongside the brightly colored vibrators that the company designs, give the space the serene air of a day spa.

Ethan Imboden, the company's founder, is forty and holds an electrical engineering degree from Johns Hopkins and a master's in industrial design from Pratt Institute. He has a thin face and blue eyes, and wears a pair of small hoop earrings beneath brown hair that is often tousled in some fashion. The first time I visited, one April morning, Imboden had on a V-neck sweater, designer jeans and Converse sneakers with the tongues splayed out—an aesthetic leaning that masks a highly programmatic interior. "I think if you asked my mother she'd probably say I lined up my teddy bears at right angles," he told me.

Imboden was seated next to a white conference table, reviewing a marketing graphic that Jimmyjane was preparing to email customers before the summer season. Projected onto a wall was an image that promoted three of Jimmyjane's vibrators, superimposed over postcards of iconic destinations—Paris, the Taj Mahal, a Mexican surf beach—with the title: "Meet Jimmyjane's Mile High Club: The perfect traveling companions for your summer adventures." The postcard for the Form 2, a vibrator Imboden created with the industrial designer Yves Behar, was pictured alongside the Eiffel Tower with the note: "Bonjour! Thanks to my handy button lock I breezed through my flight without making noise or causing an international incident. See you soon, FORM 2."

Jimmyjane's conceit is to presuppose a world in which there is no hesitation around sex toys. Placing its products on familiar cultural ground has a normalizing effect, Imboden believes, and comparing a vibrator to a lifestyle accessory someone might pack into their carry-on luggage next to an iPad shifts people's perceptions about where these objects fit into their lives. Jimmyjane products have been sold in places like C.O. Bigelow, the New York apothecary, Sephora, W Hotels, and even Drugstore.com. Insinuating beautifully designed and thoughtfully engineered sex toys into the mainstream consumer landscape could push Americans into more comfortable territory around sex in general. Jimmyjane hopes to achieve this without treading too firmly on mainstream sensibilities. "Not everyone sits in a conference room and talks about vibrators, dildos, anal sex, clitorises—and we do," Imboden explained. "It's important for us to remain a part of the mainstream culture and sensitive to how normal people discuss or don't discuss these subjects."

Ten years ago, walking into the annual sex toy industry show for the first time, Imboden was startled by the objects he encountered. He had developed DNA sequencers for government scientists at Lawrence Berkeley National Laboratory, and more recently he had left a job designing consumer products—cell phones and electric toothbrushes—for companies like Motorola and Colgate, work he found dispiriting. "It was imminently clear to me that I was creating a huge amount of landfill," Imboden told me. "I wanted no part of it." He struck out on his own, and found himself approached by a potential client about designing a sex product.

The floor of the Adult Novelty Manufacturers Expo, held that year on the windowless ground level of the Sheraton in Universal City, California, flaunted fated landfill of a different sort: a gaudy display of "severed anatomy, goofy animals, and penis-pump flashing-lights kind of stuff," Imboden recalled. These tawdry novelties dominate the $1.3 billion-a-year American sex toy market. They are the output of a small but cliquish old boys' network of companies you've probably never heard of, even if you have given business to them. One of these, Doc Johnson, was named as a mocking tribute to President Lyndon B. Johnson, whose justice department in the 1960s tried in vain to prosecute the late pornographer Reuben Sturman, the industry's notorious founding father. Sturman invented the peep show booth, and built a formidable empire of adult bookstores that for decades constituted the shadowy domain where such products were sold, usually to men.

Imboden was inspired. "As soon as I saw past the fact that in front of me happened to be two penises fused together at the base, I realized that I was looking at the only category of consumer product that had yet to be touched by design," Imboden said. "It's as if the only food that had been available was in the candy aisle, like Dum Dums and Twizzlers, where it's really just about a marketing concept and a quick rush and very little emphasis on nourishment and real enjoyment. The category had been isolated by the taboo that surrounded it. I figured, I can transcend that."

At dinner parties in San Francisco, where he lives, Imboden found that mentioning sex toys unleashed conversations that appeared to have been only awaiting permission. "Suddenly I was at the nexus of everybody's thoughts and aspirations of sexuality," he said. "Suddenly it was okay for anyone to talk to me about it." It occurred to Imboden that the people who buy sex toys are not some *other* group of people. They are among the half of all Americans who, according to a recent Indiana University study, report having used a vibrator. They are people, like those waiting outside Apple stores for the newest iPhone model, who typically surround themselves with brands that reinforce a self-concept. They spend money on quality products, and care about the safety of those products. Yet, for the very products they use most intimately—arguably the ones whose quality and safety people should care most about—they were buying gimmicky items of questionable integrity. It's just that people had never come to expect or demand anything different—silenced by society's "shame tax on sexuality," as one sex toy retailer put it to me. And few alternatives existed.

Jean-Michel Valette, the chairman of Peet's Coffee, who would later join Jimmyjane's Board of Directors, told me: "I had thought the opportunities for really transforming significant consumer categories had all been done. Starbucks had done it in coffee. Select Comfort had done it in beds. Boston Beers"—the makers of Samuel Adams—"had done it in beer. And here was one that was right under everyone's nose."

Jimmyjane's success has inspired a growing class of design-conscious companies—including Minna, Nomi Tang and Je Joue—that are beginning to clean up an unscrupulous industry long cloaked by American discomfort around sex. LELO, a Swedish brand founded by industrial designers, creates upmarket products with names—Gigi, Ina, Nea—that sound like feminized IKEA furniture. (Try Gigi on the SVELVIK bed!) OhMiBod, a line of vibrators created by a woman who once worked in Apple's product marketing department, synchronize rhythmically with iPods, iPads, iPhones and other smartphones.

I asked Imboden what qualified him to design a vibrator, a device primarily intended for female pleasure. Imboden said he considers himself "decidedly heterosexual," but also "universally perceptive," and he suspects that the formative childhood years he spent living with his mother and older sister, after his father died of cancer when he was two, may have nurtured within him a certain empathy for the opposite sex. (His father had also been an engineer, also worked at Lawrence Berkeley Laboratory, and ended up starting a dressmaking company called Foxy Lady.) "Ethan has an intellectual curiosity and an emotional maturity that doesn't stop him from exploring something that a man 'shouldn't,'" said Lisa Berman, Jimmyjane's C.E.O., who came from The Limited and Guess and is among the company's all-female executive team. "He is a real purist in the way he thinks, not just about engineering and design but the emotional connection that these products might assist in a relationship. He can do that better than anyone that I've met."

Imboden enlisted his mother and sister to help him start the company. These made for some strange moments, as in the time when his mom complimented him on a well-written description of how a vibrator could be inserted safely for anal use, calling out from across the room, "Ethan, you handled the anus beautifully." His friend Brian and other close friends invested initial seed money. Professional investors were intrigued but hesitant; here was a first-time entrepreneur, making a consumer product that was not, strictly speaking, technology (it being the Bay Area, this mattered)—and it was about sex. "They were scared of it," Imboden said. (Banks still refuse their business, citing vague "morality clauses.") Tim Draper, a prominent Silicon Valley venture capitalist known for backing ventures like Skype and Hotmail, thought differently. "He had a unique way of looking at the world, and a great sense for product design," Draper wrote to me in an email. "He understood branding."

Little Gold, Jimmyjane's first vibrator, is a slender thing that could be mistaken for a cigar case. Imboden developed and patented a replaceable motor that slides inside the twenty-four-carat gold-plated shell, which he engineered to vibrate in near silence. It is a portable, durable, and waterproof sex toy designed never to become landfill. For Imboden, it was merely a proof of concept. "It's an immediate disruption of the associations that we have with sexual products," he said.

The trendy London-based apothecary, Space.NK, bought the concept, and displayed Jimmyjane right next to Marc Jacobs's new fragrances. Soon after, Selfridges, the high-end British department store, carried the company's products. For Imboden, debuting in European retailers was a deliberate end-run around American social taboos, and also made a sidestep of the sex toy industry entirely. It was a statement that products like vibrators did not have to be relegated to their own store or a discreet web-site. Premiering in lofty precincts before trickling down to the mainstream borrowed from a fashion playbook: Little Gold could be thought of as Jimmyjane's couture offering, its runway show-piece. A more accessible aluminum version, Little Chroma, now sells for $125 at Drugstore.com.

Early on, Imboden would also hang around celebrity gath-erings, putting vibrators in the hands of influencers. After the Grammy Awards one year, he found himself walking across an in-tersection in front of a white lowrider. Inside, two heads bobbed to music; "Snoop de Ville" ran across the side of the car. As Im-boden jogged over to the front window, he reached inside his shoulder bag for a vibrator, and "it dawns on me that this is a per-fect recipe for getting shot," he recalls. Snoop Dogg was behind the wheel, talking on a cell phone; a chandelier swayed gently above him. Imboden handed him a Little Something. "This dude just gave me a twenty-four-k gold vibrator," Snoop relayed into the phone. Then he turned to Imboden. "Thank you, my nigga. I'm gonna put this to work *right now.*"

In January 2005, the Little Gold made it into the Golden Globe Awards gift suite, the freebie swag lounge that, in those days, A-list celebrities actually visited. "To have a non-fashion item like that at one of these showcases was really unusual and groundbreaking," Rose Apodaca, the West Coast bureau chief of *Women's Wear Daily* at the time, told me. "It was the hot item everyone was trying to get their hands on." Teri Hatcher and Jennifer Garner, by picking one up, became among the brand's first celebrity endorsers. Apodaca wrote about it in *WWD*'s awards season special. "Suddenly there's this tool for sex being featured in the bible of the fashion industry." After Kate Moss was spotted purchasing a Little Gold from a Greenwich Village

lingerie boutique—a "buzz-worthy bauble," Page Six wrote—
Jimmyjane appeared in *Vogue*.

After the introduction of electric lights in 1876, home appliances
were plugged in, one by one, beginning with the sewing machine
and followed by the fan, the teakettle, the toaster and then, the vibrator. (The vacuum cleaner would come ten years later.) Ads for
them appeared in *Hearst's, Popular Mechanics, Modern Women* and
Women's Home Companion, among many others. A *National Home
Journal* ad in 1908 for a five-dollar hand-powered vibrator, de-
clared: "Gentle, soothing, invigorating and refreshing. Invented
by a woman who knows a woman's needs. All nature pulsates and
vibrates with life." Another in *American Magazine* claimed that
the vibrator "will chase away the years like magic... All the keen
relish, the pleasures of youth, will throb within you... Your self-
respect, even, will be increased a hundredfold." A Sears, Roebuck
catalog in 1918 advertised a portable vibrator on a page (with fans
and household mixers) of "Aids That Every Woman Appreciates."

Was this language camouflage for an orgasm? Were these vibrators also intended, with a wink, for masturbation? This has
become the popular history of the device as written by Rachel
Maines, a Cornell researcher, who argued in her 1999 book *The
Technology of Orgasm* that electric vibrators replaced the hands of
doctors who, from the time of Hippocrates to the 1920s, had been
massaging women to orgasm as a treatment for hysteria.

Hysteria: The seventeenth-century French physician Lazare
Rivière described it as "a sort of madness, arising from a vehe-
ment and unbridled desire of carnal embracement which desire
disthrones the Rational Faculties so far, that the Patient utters
wanton and lascivious Speeches." Today, this sounds a lot like
normal functioning of female sexuality. But men long viewed it

as a disorder. During antiquity physicians believed that hysteria was caused by the womb meandering around the body, wrecking havoc, yet by the nineteenth century the term had become "the wastepaper basket of medicine where one throws otherwise unemployed symptoms," as the French physiatrist Charles Lasègue put it. (The American Psychiatric Association finally dropped hysteria altogether from the Diagnostic and Statistical Manual of Mental Disorders in 1952, the same year it added homosexuality.)

Virgins, nuns, widows and women with impotent husbands were thought especially prone. Victorian physicians, especially in England and the United States, were wary of female arousal. They viewed it as a dangerous slope towards uncontrollable desires and ill health, and advised women against tea, coffee, masturbation, feather beds, wearing tight corsets, and reading French novels.

Maines argues that relieving women of this pent-up desire was a standard medical practice. She takes us back to the Greek physician Soranus, who in the first century AD discussed his treatment: "We...moisten these parts freely with sweet oil, keeping it up for some time," he wrote. Helen King, a historian and leading authority of Classical medicine at England's Open University, told me that a correct translation of this passage has him massaging the abdomen, the typical treatment for yet another female disorder—chronic flowing of female "seed"—for which rose oil was prescribed, along with cold baths and avoiding sexy pictures. Rather, King says, it is with the influential Roman physician Galen where we see the first explicit mention of genital massage to orgasm as a medical treatment. Galen discusses a woman rubbing "the customary remedies" on her genitals—sachets of Artemisia, marjoram and iris oil—and feeling the "pain and at the same time the pleasure" associated with intercourse.

But did doctors do the deed? Probably not in antiquity, King said—there was a taboo against such things even back then, and the task was likely assigned to midwives. References in the annals of medicine to genital massage are oblique, leaving a trove of circumstantial evidence, with some exceptions, like the British physician Nathaniel Highmore complaining in the seventeenth century that massaging the vulva was "not unlike that game of boys in which they try to rub their stomachs with one hand and pat their heads with the other." Maines believes that doctors considered this a tedious task, and not a sexual act, since sexual relations, especially in those pre-Clinton centuries, meant proper intercourse. However, if intercourse failed to relieve the symptoms of desire—only recently have we known that up to 70 percent of women cannot reach orgasm from intercourse alone—doctors prescribed hydrotherapy (the douche sprays in Saratoga Springs, NY, were a popular destination for women whose husbands were at the racetrack) or an office visit.

In 1869, an American physician, George Taylor, patented a steam-powered contraption called the "Manipulator," in which a patient lay stomach-down on a padded table and received a pelvis massage from a vibrating sphere. The Chattanooga, a 125-pound apparatus that sold in 1904 for $200, was used on both sexes for various treatments including, the company's catalog described, "female troubles." All manner of inventions were marketed to doctors: musical vibrators, vibratory forks, vibrating wire coils called vibratiles, floor-standing models on rollers and portable devices shaped like hair dryers. They were powered by air pressure, water turbines, gas engines and batteries. We don't really know how common the practice of massaging women with these devices actually was—Maines's book touched off a debate among sex historians, with some arguing that it was probably rare and considered quack medicine—but in any case, after the first electromechanical vibrator was patented in 1880, vibrators marketed for home use flourished. General Electric and Hamilton Beach both made handheld devices that looked like hair dryers, boxed with various attachments. (I recently found a 1902 Hamilton Beach vibrator listed on eBay for $25.99.) Women could now regain the "pleasures of youth" through their own devices.

For reasons that are not entirely clear, vibrator ads gradually disappeared from upmarket magazines after the 1920s, and went underground. Fifty years later they would resurface—Hitachi's Magic Wand Massager first appeared in the 1970s and remains one of the top-selling vibrators, even though the company will tell you it doesn't make vibrators—and feminists in New York City began teaching women self-pleasure. By the 1990s, Bob Dole was talking about erectile dysfunction as the pitchman for Viagra, and the Starr Report described fellatio and a semen-stained dress, pushing the boundaries of acceptable mainstream media conversation.

And then, Miranda presented Charlotte with the Rabbit Pearl, a pink, phallus-shaped vibrator with rotating beads and animated bunny ears, on prime-time cable television.

Everyone in the sex toy business with whom I spoke credits "Sex and the City" with profoundly changing the way Americans now talk about sex toys. The Rabbit Pearl became an overnight sensation—"Talk about product placement," the vibrator's manufacturer, Dan Martin of Vibratex, told me. With clean, well-lit stores like Good Vibrations and Babeland; the Tupperware-inspired, sex-toy house gatherings for women known as Pleasure Parties ("Where Every Day is Valentine's Day"); and the Internet—which opened all kinds of new avenues for sexual adventure—women now had safe and discreet places to buy it. The Rabbit

Pearl is still the top-selling sex toy, although the original from Vibratex has been knocked off so many times that "the rabbit" has become generic.

In an episode during the fifth season of "Sex and the City," Samantha walks into a Sharper Image to return her vibrator.

"We don't sell vibrators," the clerk tells her.

"Yes you do, I bought this here six months ago," Samantha replies, holding up the device.

"That's not a vibrator," he says, "that's a neck massager."

Within Sharper Image, that neck massager became known jokingly as "the 'Sex and the City' vibrator," but in 2007, Imboden approached the company with the Form 6. Literally the sixth in a series of vibrator sketches—Imboden believes in minimalist names—the Form 6 has a curved, organic shape that is suggestive without being representational. It is wrapped completely in soft, platinum silicone, making it completely water-resistant, and charges on a wall-powered base station through a narrow stainless steel band, a novel cordless recharging system that Imboden patented. For these features, the Form 6 earned an International Design Excellence Award, the first time a sex toy had earned such a distinction. It comes in hot pink, deep plum or slate—non-primary, poppy colors that he believes convey sophistication. It is packaged in a hard plastic case inside a bright white box—"literally and figuratively bringing these products out of the shadows," Imboden said. And it has a three-year warranty (this may not seem remarkable, but is for a sex toy).

"It was certainly controversial internally," recalled Adam Ertel, Sharper Image's buyer at the time. Sharper Image decided to try the Form 6 in a few stores—"a waterproof personal massager" is how they described it—and, to everyone's surprise, the Form 6 soon became one of the retailer's best-selling massage items. They quickly rolled it out nationwide. "It was clear to all of us that we were treading on new ground," said Ertel. "We realized that the people that bought the Form 6 for its intimate nature may be a large group of consumers that people aren't strategically selling to."

One afternoon in May, I joined Imboden at a meeting with Yves Behar to talk through ideas for the Form 4, their next vibrator. They met at Behar's downtown San Francisco design studio, fuseproject, around a conference table topped with some rudimentary prototypes that they would pick up and flex in different directions while discussing "torque" and "harmonics" and "programming sequences." On a counter along the back wall stood a desk lamp that Behar designed for Herman Miller. Behar is perhaps best known for creating the One Laptop Per Child computer and perhaps least known for designing both New York City's branded bike helmet and its official condom dispenser. The two had been friends for a while—Behar was an early advisor to Jimmyjane—before deciding, a couple years ago, to collaborate. "Isn't this that old-fashioned *Playboy* mansion cliché, two guys coming up with products used for women?" Behar asked. "I don't know if it is because I have twenty-plus years experience of design or thirty years of sexual experiences. You put the two together and you can get to some really interesting places."

During the initial brainstorms, which included the women on their respective teams, some awkward workplace conversations, and plenty of giggling, Imboden and Behar identified three different functions that a vibrator should deliver. They decided to roll them out in a trio of devices—a collection they've named "Pleasure to the People"—all built upon a modular base structure that houses a common digital interface, wireless rechargeable battery and motor. They designed the Form 2, their first product, to be a "new interpretation" of the Rabbit Pearl. Its form is compact, resting ergonomically in the palm of the hand, with a novel shape that resembles a padded tuning fork or a portly, marshmallow Peep Easter bunny—suggestive enough of the iconic Rabbit to appear familiar to people, but amorphous enough that they don't dwell too much on what it looks like. "It's not just a lumpy random shape," Imboden pointed out. "I think there's a real sense of purpose in the forms which communicate that this is not an arbitrary act or a whimsical random thing we've created."

Through their design, Imboden wants to convey the sense that these are carefully considered objects—that someone is looking out for our sexual well-being, even if we have been conditioned to have low expectations. "I jokingly say this is an area where you really don't want to disappoint your customers," Behar told me. "And I think this is an industry that has treated its customers really badly." The Form 2 takes a symmetrical, organic form but they avoid emulating anatomy, because while "the penis is very well designed to accomplish what it needs to accomplish, a vibrator doesn't actually need to do those same things," Imboden said. One function it was not designed to accomplish was to stimulate a woman's G-spot, but even if it did, mimicking male genitalia treads on psychological territory that Imboden would rather avoid. "While on the one hand that has its own excitement, there becomes a third person," he said, noting that some men feel threatened by an object they perceive to be a substitution for themselves. "People aren't necessarily seeking to have a threesome. Our goal has really been for the focus to be on you and your sensations and the interaction with your partner and not really to pull attention to the product itself. That's an element of why we make the products as quiet as they are. It's also why we make them visually quiet." Representational objects, like taxidermy hanging in a lodge, take up psychic space; figurative forms leave fantasy open to one's own interpretation. "Staying away from body shapes," Imboden explained, "is a way of keeping open provocative possibility, as opposed to narrowing it down to a provocative prescription."

The Form 3, the second vibrator designed with Behar, has a vibrating, ultra-thin soft silicone skin that flexes into the curve of the palm. The Form 4, the two men discussed that afternoon, should "deliver an oomph." Imboden believed they could achieve this by setting two motors to vibrate at different frequencies. Behar pondered an internal structure that would allow the vibrator to bend in various directions, similar to the neck of his Herman Miller lamp. "Plus it makes it look exactly like Barbapapa, my childhood hero," he said, referring to the popular French cartoon creature that looks like a pear-shaped blob and can change shape. "For each of these projects we came up with some funny metaphors," he told me. "It keeps you true to the original concept."

From a study released in 2009 by Indiana University, the first academic, peer-reviewed study to look at vibrator use, we now know that 53 percent of women and nearly half of all men in the United States have used a vibrator. This makes it nearly as common an appliance in American households as the drip coffeemaker or toaster oven, *The New York Times* reported, and about twice as prevalent among American adults as condoms, according to Church & Dwight, maker of Trojan condoms, which funded the Indiana University study. Jimmyjane's own sales reveal that as many men as women, as many twenty-five-year-olds as fifty-year olds, and as many Virginians as Californians, per capita, are buying vibrators. At each phase of life, a sex toy might take on new meaning; perhaps, initially, as a way to explore one's own body, but later, within a long-term relationship, as a way to sustain excitement. Today sex therapists are hearing more discussion of what they call "desire discrepancies"—one partner wanting sex more, or less, or in a different manner, than the other. "Our bread and butter used to be orgasm and erection problems," said Sandor Gardos, a sex therapist, adding that self-help sources and Viagra have arisen to address those issues. "There's more discussion now around the subtle and complex issues of relationship and sexuality."

Imboden sees Jimmyjane as playing into that discussion around sex and well-being, not only as a peddler of "marital aids"—terminology still used by the handful of online sex-toy retailers catering to religious Christians—but as a trusted provocateur. Guests looking for condoms at W Hotels will find Jimmyjane's Pocket Pleasure Set in their room's minibar, a slim package containing condoms, a mini-vibrator, a feather tickler, and the "love decoder"—a piece of paper folded like an Origami fortune-teller that engages players in titillating acts through a game of chance. "Everybody wants to try these new boundaries but they need a catalyst to make this happen," Imboden told me. "We are granting them permission by transferring the responsibility to us."

One day, I flew to Los Angeles with Imboden for a routine trip he was taking to different retailers that carry Jimmyjane. We started at Hustler Hollywood, an upmarket sex emporium on a corner of the Sunset Strip, with a glass façade, bright lights and polished floors. Hard-core pornography was displayed just feet from an in-store coffee bar, arguably two things that should occupy different spaces, but the suggestion is to get over it. Presenting erotica stigma-free in the manner of a Barnes & Noble triggers the disorienting feel of a dark nightclub suddenly flooded with fluorescent ceiling lights, where everyone can see what you've been doing in the corner. But a fishbowl is precisely the metaphor of transparency Larry Flynt had in mind, and amidst this forthright statement of normalized sexuality (store motto: "Relax...it's just sex"), Jimmyjane is at home.

"With most other consumer products, like a pair of jeans, you have to convince people *why* they need it," Cory Silverberg, a certified sex educator and author who writes the "Sexuality Guide" for About.com, had told me. "With sex toys people come in already interested, and what you are doing is removing the obstacles. A lot of it is permission giving—saying that sex toys don't make you kinky, or that your boyfriend or girlfriend isn't good enough."

Imboden told me that Jimmyjane was the first to present sex toys in white packaging, and that retailers, accustomed to the candy-colored aesthetic, told him customers would never go for it. Several packages made by the company's competitors now have a cleaner, white look. Imboden picked one of them off a rack, and pointed out the words bullet-pointed on the package: *body-safe materials, phthalate-free, waterproof.* "You never used to see that," he said. European laws have driven much of the industry's attention to materials safety, but whether it is to be believed is something different. Sander Gardos, who founded MyPleasure.com, an on-line retailer of sex toys, had told me, "You cannot trust what's on the box—it has nothing to do with what's actually in there," recalling a manufacturer at a trade show in Shanghai who stood before a display of two boxes that contained the same product—one was labeled "100% TPR" (thermoplastic rubber), the other "100% silicone"—and then admitted both were made with PVC. "We have visited the Chinese factories that make all the toys that say 'Made in Japan,'" Gardos said. "There are tremendous quality-control issues in this industry because it is completely unregulated."

A stand-alone glass case carried what the salesman distinguished as the "sex devices"—superior quality, more nicely designed and higher priced products "that don't crap out," as he put it. Jimmyjane's products occupied two shelves. The case also displayed products by LELO and Minna. On another shelf was OhMiBod's Freestyle vibrator, which pulsates to music from an mp3 player. It bore a striking resemblance to the Form 6, down to its solid plum color and narrow metallic band.

Nearby, in West Hollywood, we stopped in at Coco de Mer, a luxury erotic boutique with outlets in London and Manhattan. With Dave Stewart of the Eurythmics, who is an investor in the store, Imboden designed a custom version of the Little Chroma in black, with Stewart's lyrics etched into the aluminum and a leather cord threaded through the cap, along with a custom guitar pick. We then met Robin Coe-Hutshing at Studio BeautyMix, her store inside Fred Segal, in Santa Monica (which has since changed ownership). A wall behind the custom fragrance counter displayed Jimmyjane's vibrators, white porcelain massage stones (for which it won an International Design Excellence Award), and scented massage oil candles, which were the first candles of any kind to be formulated with a melting point matching body temperature, an innovation that makes them an effective emollient when poured onto the skin. In an environment of soaps, perfumes and skin cream, Jimmyjane's bright color palette and white boxes fit as seamlessly as they had in a room of maid outfits and butt plugs. If Hustler Hollywood and Studio BeautyMix might represent almost dichotomous approaches to sex—the excitement of sexual fantasy versus the everyday made sexy—Jimmyjane works in both worlds by remaining agnostic.

We finished our tour in Venice, at A+R, the design store that Rose Apodaca, the former *Women's Wear Daily* editor, opened with her husband Andy Griffith. The store displays a compendium of home accessories from designers around the world. The Form 2 sits on a shelf behind glass in a wall display next to the Braun travel alarm clock by Dieter Rams, and is sometimes mistaken by customers, according to Apodaca, for a Japanese anime toy. In the adjacent case, beside colored glass vases in the shape of honey bears, are the Form 6 and Little Chroma. "We wanted to include these products in our mix because we wanted it to seem like a perfectly normal part of one's lifestyle," Apodaca told me. "Just like they'd have a great wine carafe or a filtered water bottle." When Sasha Baron Cohen walked into the store the week before I visited and learned what that Little Chroma was, he proceeded to browse the store picking up random objects and asking, "Does this vibrate?"

Victoria's Secret, a $5 billion retailer ubiquitous today in American shopping malls, was founded in San Francisco in the 1970s by a Stanford Business School graduate who felt embarrassed buying lingerie for his wife in a department store, and set out to create a more inviting atmosphere for men. Soon, picking up a vibrator in a shopping mall, or a store that sells home accessories, cosmetics or lattes may seem rather conventional. It nearly is already. One of the faster growing categories in terms of sales at Walgreen's, the nation's biggest drugstore chain, is sexual wellness. Walgreens has been selling a vibrating ring—a gateway sex toy—made by Trojan, since 2006, except in the seven U.S. states where it is illegal to do so; Target and Wal-Mart sell them as well. Amazon.com currently carries just under eighty thousand sexual wellness products. Sales of "sexual enhancement devices" in mass food and drug retailers (excluding Wal-Mart) increased by 20 percent for the year that ended April 15, according to

Symphony IRI Group, a Chicago-based market-research firm. Yearly sales of sexual products through home-party direct sales, like Pleasure Parties, are more than $400 million. "Vibrators are already mainstream," said Jim Daniels, Trojan's former vice president for marketing, who estimates the market for vibrators in the United States to be $1 billion—more than twice that of condoms.

Trojan, along with Durex and Lifestyle, are among the large companies now developing vibrators that a place like Walgreen's might start to feel okay about selling under florescent lights. Trojan has introduced the sixty-dollar Vibrating Twister—the condom maker's third vibrator model. For a trial, Philips Electronics launched a line of "intimate massagers" under their Relationship Care category. "These big multinational companies are realizing there is a ton money to be made," says Cory Silverberg. "They will change things more significantly than the political feminist sex stores and some of the more interesting manufacturers like Jimmyjane." Mainstream manufacturers and retailers are couching these products as being good for sexual health—that it's not just about getting turned on, or being kinky, but about being healthy, like exercising and eating well. "That's not exactly a change in our comfort with sex," says Silverberg—it still will be some time before sex toy ads become as acceptable as Viagra commercials—"it's a marketing ploy, but it will give people permission to try something they want to try anyway."

Johnson & Johnson's KY relaunched its own brand with what it's calling "intimacy enhancing products for couples," including a topical female arousal gel "scientifically proven to enhance a woman's intimate satisfaction." "I look at it as the final frontier of the women's movement," says Dr. Laura Berman, a prominent TV sex and relationships therapist who incited a vibrator buying frenzy after appearing on "Oprah" with various devices.

"Women now feel more entitled and free to explore their own sexual responses."

As sex toys become just another personal electronic device, our expectations of them and how they are used are bound to change. Imboden has been considering this scenario for years already, quietly developing technologies that he says will "fundamentally alter the way that we interact with these products." Imagine wearable sensors—embedded in clothing, or a bracelet—that operate according to heart rate, blood pressure and skin response. Imagine devices that communicate via a personal area network, connecting sexual partners in ways they don't even realize.

One afternoon at Jimmyjane's offices, Imboden told me that he believed the companies that will succeed in making sex toys are those that are forthright, trusted and accountable, like an intimate partner. He paused, then added—"and give great orgasms"—just before it became an afterthought.

Sex by Numbers
Rachel Swan

Jessica, John and Kate (not their real names) sat together at Cafe Van Kleef recently, looking more like three longtime friends than three people involved in a love triangle—or, as they'd put it, a love polygonal. Jessica had an arm casually draped around John, who leaned against her contentedly. The two of them met on OKCupid about three years ago, started an email correspondence, and hooked up, for the first time, at a friend's Christmas party—John says they spent most of it making out in the bathroom. They started seeing each other "in a fling capacity," he says, and fell in love against their better interests. John clearly remembers the day it struck him: "We were outside a Virgin Megastore in New York," he recalled, "next to two guys who were laying asphalt. I suddenly turned to her and I was like, 'Hey, I love you.' And she started crying."

About a year into their relationship, Kate entered the picture.

She and John had actually known each other for a long time, and John said they'd always had a lot of chemistry. Both were warm and loquacious, identified as "queer," and saw themselves as part of the Bay Area's sexual underground. They'd actually met at a drag show. One day, Kate showed up at a music event that John had produced in Oakland's Mosswood Park. (By day, he works as a freelance lighting designer for rock shows.) Kate marched straight up to Jessica. "Full disclosure," she said. "I'm only here to get in your boyfriend's pants."

Weirdly enough, it worked. It turns out Jessica is one of the few people in the world who would take kindly to someone trying to steal her man. Because she doesn't think of it as stealing; it's more like sharing. A good boyfriend shouldn't be squandered on one person, right? At this point, Kate and John have been sleeping together for a full year. They use condoms. John and Jessica are still "primary" partners. Jessica, in the meantime, started seeing three other guys. It's not about getting even, she says; it's about sharing the love. She and Kate are best friends. And Kate has a fiancé of her own.

Confused yet? Jessica explains it this way: "So here's a conventional relationship," she said. "You meet someone, you date, after six months, you use the *L* word." She paused and glanced over at Kate, who nodded approvingly. "Then you wait for him to ask you to marry him. Then you have a baby."

That isn't what she ever wanted. In fact, since reading Dossie Easton's polyamory primer, *The Ethical Slut*, in college, Jessica decided that she wanted to impose a cooperative, communal model on her own romantic life, without being a total freak. Although her current relationship with John is her first real foray into polyamory, Jessica said it's something she always wanted. She's certainly not inured to jealousy—no one is, she argues—but she's found ways to sublimate it. And she feels that the returns are well worth the sacrifice, adding that she'll probably never go back to old one-on-one style partnership. "I *like* being a slut," she insisted.

And Jessica's not alone. Over the past decade, polyamory has gone from being a fringe trend to a bona fide scene to a relationship model that's widespread enough to almost be socially acceptable. The scene has its own canon, which includes texts like *The Ethical Slut* and Christopher Ryan's *Sex at Dawn* (coauthored with his wife, Cacilda Jetha). Plus it's got celebrities like alt-weekly sex columnist Dan Savage, who coined the word *monogamish* and turned open relationships into a cause célèbre. He's currently shooting a late-night advice show for MTV. Some would even argue that the proliferation of social networks and dating sites—namely, Facebook and OKCupid—has turned us into a more open culture. The Bay Area in particular, with its long history of free love, its vast network of Burning Man enthusiasts, and its overall progressive ethos, is a natural hotbed for the alternative sex scene. It's a place where avid polyamorists can bring just about anyone into their fold.

Sort of. It turns out that, no matter how successful they've been at negotiating relationships, many polyamorists still have one foot in the closet. And in a world where monogamy is not only well entrenched but vital to the workings of a property-based society, their scene may always remain marginal.

That realization has caused many "ethical sluts" to treat open relationships not only as a lifestyle but as a social cause.

Christopher Ryan has spent most of the last ten years combating what he calls "the standard narrative": that man's nature is to always be concerned about paternity. He started writing *Sex at Dawn* about eleven years ago as a PhD dissertation. At that time, Ryan was studying psychology at Saybrook University and working at a San Francisco nonprofit called Women in Community Service. "It was all women, except for me and one other guy," Ryan said, "and they were all lesbian-feminist Berkeley types."

Ryan was in the midst of reading Robert Wright's *The Moral Animal*, which uses evolutionary psychology to figure out whether men are congenital cheaters. Ryan had a major hard-on for the book. He'd recap Wright's theories for anyone who would listen, including the women at his nonprofit—who mostly dismissed them. "They said, 'That sounds really Victorian and phallocentric,'" Ryan recalled. He didn't take their criticisms as insult. Rather, he decided to go back and explore some of Wright's original research.

And that led him to the bonobos. Ryan contends that if you want to challenge the standard narrative of human sexuality, you can't just start at the beginning of civilization—you have to go all the way back to our primate ancestors. He explained it thus to a crowd of roughly a dozen acolytes at San Francisco's Center for Sex and Culture: "If your dog shits on your bed, and you want to know why, you're not going to study birds. You're going to look at wolves, and foxes, and coyotes." Similarly, if your girlfriend sleeps around, and you want to know why, take a look at the female bonobos at the San Diego Zoo. As Ryan's friend Carol Queen pointed out, you'll see a lot of parents at the zoo covering their children's eyes: bonobos love to hump.

There's really no way to answer an essential question about human evolution without resorting to conjecture, so Ryan and his coauthor (and wife) Jetha tried to have some humility about it. They also tried to incorporate data from as many disciplines as possible—primatology, archaeology, nutritional biology, psychology, contemporary sexuality, pornography, you name it.

They drew some interesting conclusions: first and foremost, that monogamy really began with the advent of agriculture. That's when we became concerned about ownership and possession. That's when men decided that the only way to uphold a property-based society was to control women's bodies. In Ryan's estimation, it didn't take that long—evolutionarily speaking—for us to invent the phrase "Thou shalt not covet thy neighbor's wife."

But there's more. Ryan and Jetha also discovered some interesting and oft-maligned facets of female sexuality that were borne out in bonobo research. Namely, that women are raving perverts, that they're way more "bisexual" than men, and that they make a lot more noise during sex. Even more importantly: we're all perverts. Or, as Ryan would put it, we're "promiscuous" beings—promiscuous not in the sense of prurience, but in the sense of wanting to mix, being fiercely egalitarian and wanting to have sex with as many different people as possible.

We've been taught to think in terms of competition and scarcity, Ryan says, meaning that we're told if we don't ensnare one partner within a certain time frame, our chance at reproduction will run out. He contends that this line of thinking is culturally imposed, and that in reality, we're not thinking about procreation every time we have sex—we're doing it for pleasure. "Think about the number of times you've had sex," Ryan said to the audience at Center for Sex and Culture. He paused, allowing us to mentally calculate. "Now divide that by the number of kids you have." A few people chortled, though some hid their faces uncomfortably. Point taken.

Ryan isn't particularly doctrinal—he purposefully left the pedagogical, thumb-sucking, "Where to go from here" chapter out of *Sex at Dawn*. But his book, which quickly landed on the *New York Times* bestseller list, has become a de facto bible in the polyamory community. John and Jessica both invoke his theories when trying to define their relationship. "Monogamy automatically assumes all these rules," Jessica said. That's why, when you desire someone besides your one life partner, it's called "cheating."

John would venture even farther, arguing that open relationships are actually a more natural state than marriage and the nuclear family. "Okay, like ten percent of people in this society say they're gay, right? I think about the same amount of people are naturally born monogamous." He continued: "But from day one, as a society, we're immediately routed toward monogamy. This shit starts right when you get out of the womb, man. Wrap that colored blanket around them, put the mother and father on the birth certificate. Boom."

He's rankled about that. "The whole 'It takes a village' thing? It shouldn't be a foreign concept." John added that Ryan's book merely validated feelings he's had for years. "It helped me find words to express how I function." John will readily admit that his parents were monogamous, and that he grew up without any kind of progressive, open relationship model to use as a reference point. Nonetheless, he says he's been poly his whole life.

One of the people who attended Ryan's lecture was Polly Whittaker, a slender, freckled blond who is a veritable Johnny Appleseed of the local polyamory community. Whittaker is one of those rare people who can flaunt her sexual preferences without compunction, since she works in the alt-sex world full time. Born in the United Kingdom and raised in a fairly permissive family—her parents were both sex therapists, and her mother "turned a blind eye" to her father's multiple affairs—she started going to fetish clubs as a teenager, immersed herself in the "sex underground," and entered her first open relationship after immigrating to the

United States in 1999. "The first weekend I came was the Folsom Street Fair," she said. "It was amazing. I was like, 'Yay, this is my town, I've arrived.'"

Some people only recognize Whittaker by the costumes she wears at sex parties, which involve a lot of pink wigs and corsets. In person, though, she's polite and down-to-business, and exudes a surprisingly small amount of sexual energy. In fact, she looks like a grown-up version of the Swiss Miss hot chocolate logo: cute, fair-skinned, and much younger in appearance than her thirty-six years. She says that by day she's focused on writing; her partner, Scott Levkoff, is a puppeteer.

The couple launched their organization, Mission Control, in January 2001, after leasing a second-floor walk-up in the Mission. Whittaker already had her own fetish party, but she wanted to increase the clientele. "I was inviting some raver-Burner types, as well," she said, indicating that the idea of mixing those subcultures was still a little outré at that time. "Those communities really hadn't crossed yet. It was like the goths were the fetish people and the ravers were the ecstasy people. There was no crossover."

Whittaker took it upon herself to bring the disparate tribes together, if only for the sake of throwing better parties. The result, she said, was fantastic: "colorful, costumed, sex-positive, Burning Man-oriented (but not Burning Man). We just created this space where people felt like they could explore."

The club now hosts seven different play parties, in addition to a monthly art salon. John said it runs the gamut: fairy nights, ladies' nights, heavier play nights, lighter play nights, trans nights, fetish nights, sex club—oriented nights. Most events cost thirty to thirty-five dollars and entail a mandatory dress code. Some require all participants to bring a buddy. "You know," he said, "they want to keep the riffraff out."

John explained that when sex parties aren't properly policed, they can attract a bad element—i.e., "dudes in sweatpants who like to jerk off while watching trannies fuck. I mean, not that it's bad to watch trannies fuck—that's hot," he said. "Sweatpants? Not so hot."

Mission Control's flagship party is called Kinky Salon, which is kind of an omnisexual catchall. It's not polyamorous per se, but you have to be poly-friendly to go, given all the exchanging of partners that happens there. According to people who go, it looks nondescript from the outside—just a grate and a door-tender. But the inside is all razzle-dazzle: wood paneling, a smokers' porch, tapestries, a dance floor with a stripper pole and mirrored disco ball, bartenders who hold your drinks (Kinky Salon has a BYOB policy and no liquor license), baskets full of condoms and lube, a back room full of beds and box springs and futons, people walking around in various stages of undress. Every iteration of the party has a theme (e.g., "woodland creatures," "superheroes," or "San Fransexual").

John has a fairly sunny view of Kinky Salon, at least in terms of its ability to attract a wide and representative swath of the poly-amory subculture. Yes, more than half of the folks who attend are white, college-educated people in their thirties, he said. But they constitute the scene's demographic majority. "It's definitely a have-your-life-together-but-are-still-having-tons-of-fun kind of crowd," he said, adding that in general, the racial makeup pretty much mirrors that of San Francisco.

Jessica's read is a little more cynical. She's been to two Mission Control parties and says they definitely stand out in a scene that's become larger and more diffuse—in the last decade, so-called "pansexual" and "alternative adult" clubs have cropped up all over San Francisco, and many of them are a little less discriminating, in terms of the crowds they draw. All the same, she finds the crowd to be pretty specific, not so much in an elitist way as in an isolationist way. And generally, it's dominated by nerds. "You know, Burning Man people, Renn Faire people, people who are really costumed," she said. "They're older. They're not really people I'm interested in fucking."

She continued: "There's this back room where you go to have sex, and there's always this weird pile of people going at it in the middle of the room. But it's way less creepy than it could be."

Ned Mayhem, a PhD student in the sciences and second-generation polyamorist (his father also has an open marriage), would agree with that assessment. He and his partner, Maggie Mayhem, have a porn website based around their "sex geek" personae. They even invented something called a PSIgasm, which uses sensory devices to measure the strength of orgasms. (They're trying to get money to develop it, but haven't been able to work within normal fund-raising apparatuses—Kickstarter snubbed them.) Mayhem said that a lot of the people he meets in the so-called "sexual underground" are nerds in other parts of their lives—grad students, engineers, costume-party types, bookworms, live-action role players. They tend to be open-minded and well educated, but always a little to the left of what mainstream society would consider "sexy."

Perhaps that explains why polyamory has formed such a flourishing, albeit circumscribed subculture. It's a scene where square pegs and misfits can reinvent themselves as Lotharios, where a self-described "socially well-adjusted" person like Jessica feels like an outlier.

Certainly, not all polyamorists attend sex parties or engage in kink—many who subscribe to the "open relationship" philosophy still consider themselves fairly vanilla. But the fact that San

Francisco has such a vast and well-networked sexual underground benefits them, too, since it makes for a more tolerant environment. It also shows that the alt-sex scene, and by extension, the polyamory scene, isn't just a countercultural fluke.

At the end of the day, though, it remains marginal. And if you buy into Ryan's argument that an ownership-based society organizes itself around monogamous relationships, then polyamory may never really become mainstream. It's a fringe movement by its very definition, and some adherents would prefer that it stay that way.

In fact, there are two main obstacles facing the polyamory movement. One is that, like it or not, we're a morality-obsessed culture, and in many ways we're still a doctrinal culture. A 2009 Gallup poll showed that 92 percent of Americans think that having an extramarital affair is morally wrong. That's about twice as many as those who condemn gay and lesbian relationships, and three times as many as those who oppose the death penalty. Which is to say that as a culture, we're intractably wedded to the idea of a solid matrimonial bond. We're more amenable to the idea of legally killing someone than the idea of wrecking a marriage.

Thus, open relationships have a long way to go before becoming socially acceptable, let alone part of the status quo. Bigots who still find the idea of gay marriage unsavory probably won't cotton to nonmonogamy anytime soon.

Most of the people interviewed for this article wanted to conceal their identities, either because they feared repercussions at work—Kate, for instance, is an elementary schoolteacher; Ned asked that the name of his university be redacted, to avoid raising the attention of administrators—or because they hadn't "come out" to their families. Jessica said her mom mildly disapproves of open relationships and tends to dodge the subject when Jessica brings it up. A woman named Jess Young, who grew up in Texas and moved to the Bay Area after college, said her parents threw her out of the house when she was in high school for being a lesbian. "I think that polyamory would be beyond the scope of their understanding," she said.

The other problem is that humans are jealous creatures, whether or not you throw the concept of ownership into the equation. Asked if we can ever overcome jealousy, Dan Savage had a pretty straightforward answer: "No," he wrote, in an email interview. "And I say that as someone who has been in a monoga-m*ish* relationship for a dozen years. Jealousy is a control, I think, a natural human emotion—just like the desire for variety and other partners."

And the truth is that polyamorous relationships are hard. Those who practice them say there's no set way of doing it. Levkoff and Whittaker are loose enough and trusting enough to let each other spend entire weekends with their respective lovers. Whittaker said she usually likes to meet the people her partner dates, particularly if it's more than just a casual romance, but she's not always interested in hearing all the details.

Jessica and John have a more hands-on approach, meaning they pretty much tell each other everything. Jessica confessed that she finds herself getting jealous in unexpected ways, and not always about sex. "I'll be like, 'Hey, you made dinner with her? No fair.'" Ned describes his relationship with Maggie as "poly-fuckerous" rather than polyamorous, and says that largely owes to time constraints; he's a full-time student, she has a day job, and neither of them has the energy for endless "processing."

Some polyamorists subscribe to the idea of "compersion,"

which is basically a way of being happy that your partner is happy, even if that means allowing your partner to see other people. Oft described as "the inverse of jealousy," it's defined both as an enlightened, empathic state, and a tool to surmount the feelings of possessiveness and insecurity that normally crop up in romantic relationships. Some polyamory scholars argue that compersion can be learned. Easton discusses it at length in *The Ethical Slut*. Jessica says she's been able to implement it sometimes. "Really," she said, "nobody's immune to jealousy."

And then, well, there's the problem of some people being liars, no matter what situation you put them in—closed, open, whatever. People in monogamous relationships cheat, but so do people in polyamorous relationships. Some people "open up" relationships in order to sabotage rather than enhance them. Savage put it bluntly: "Some people convince their partners to open their relationships, and promise them that it's not because they're not attracted to 'em anymore, but they're really done and want out of the relationship, and 'openness' for them means 'I'm out there auditioning potential new partners and as soon as I find one I'm going to dump the person I'm with.'"

Kate agreed. "Nonmonogamous people can cheat," she said. "It's just about being a dishonest schmuck. If you do it right, it's supposed to be thoughtful. You're supposed to do a lot of 'checking in' and talking things to death."

And, granted, people in polyamorous relationships deal with their fair share of dishonest schmucks. "The first guy I dated in New York, I think he wanted to rescue me from John," Jessica said. "He was super emotionally intimate with me, listened to me talk about my relationships, sort of alluded to the fact that he wasn't really down with the program. After two months he disappeared." She sighed. "I feel like dudes think that because you already have a boyfriend, they don't have to actually break things off."

John's been jilted, too. "There was a girl I was dating for a month or two, the sex was really hot, and she was down with the fact that I had another partner," he said. "Then I went off to New York for a few weeks, and she basically started dating someone who wanted to be monogamous." So the girl just bounced, leaving John in the lurch. "It really hurts when someone starts dating you, and then they have to stop because they're not actually poly." He explained that even though most people are theoretically born nonmonogamous, few people can actually practice nonmonogamy in a healthy, fair, fully communicative way. We're so habituated to think of romance in terms of competition and scarcity that it becomes nearly impossible to break away from that model. John said one would think that his and Jessica's pool of potential partners is a lot bigger than that of the average person, but it's actually more limited.

In the end, it's hard to say which model is better, given our social circumstances. "I think monogamy has certain pressures and discontents that complicate relationships," Savage wrote. "And I think polyamory does, too. You get to pick your poison."

It's possible to make a serious mess of a polyamorous relationship, be an unthinking, uncaring jerk, and alienate the people around you. Then again, it's also possible to create the kind of romance that John and Jessica apparently have, in which everything seems beautiful and clean.

Very Legal: Sex and Love in Retirement
Alex Morris

Sally loves her boyfriend Albert's hair. She loves his face and his body, too, but she keeps coming back to the hair. It is great hair, thick and luxuriant and combed back from his face in little waves that puff out here and there. Still, when they first met, Sally wasn't always sure Al was right for her. She thought, *Albert is good-looking, but he's too loud and boisterous for me.* His voice would carry across the entire dining room.

For his part, Al noticed Sally right away. He didn't sit with her at meals, but he got in the habit of stopping by her table, where he would stand and chat with the ladies seated around it. Then he joined the poker game she played every night and saw how other men flirted with her over their cards. Still, he kept his cool and waited patiently. "I used to say, 'See you at the game,' and that's all. I never made a play at her." Eventually, his slow-burn approach had the desired effect.

"He's so handsome," Sally now coos. We're in the Large Activities Room of Flushing House—an independent-living facility in Queens, with a population just over three hundred—and despite the game of volleyball going on behind them in which fifteen or so seated residents bat a balloon back and forth over a low net, Al and Sally have scooted their chairs close together, and their hands are like moths, constantly flittering over the armrests and toward each other. "He is a handsome man for eighty-nine. Look at that hair." Sally runs her fingers through it.

"And the moustache? You don't like the moustache?" asks Al.

"I love the moustache. You know that, Albert."

"You're the prettiest girl here, Sally. The prettiest woman here."

"I'm ninety years old! The prettiest girl here?" Sally laughs at the thought, and yet her hand reaches up to smooth her peach-tinted bob.

By Flushing House standards, Sally and Al took things at a glacial pace. So did Kitty and David, who had been at Flushing House together for around a year before they started dating, though she'd had a tendency to fall asleep sitting next to him in the lobby with her head resting on his shoulder. ("She came after me" is how he explains it. "It may be true," she responds.) Herb and Henrietta met in the hallway shortly after she moved in four doors down from him, and she says, "He didn't give me a chance to look for anybody else." Tony and Alice became "companions" after dancing together at the New Year's Eve party just a few months after he became a resident.

This last coupling was a particular disappointment to a number of the single women. Tony has a twinkly, Frank Sinatra vibe. He walks without a cane. He dances with panache. But while Tony will amiably two-step with anyone, his real attentions are directed at Alice, for reasons even he can't articulate. ("It just grows, I guess.") She's the one he takes on walks, the one whose hand he holds, the one he cares for ever since her memory started to slip—and the one whom he might do a few more intimate things with, though as a rule he stays tight-lipped on that particular subject.

Al decidedly doesn't. "I'm eighty-nine, but I've still got that zing." Along with chewing gum and sugar pills, he keeps Viagra in a plastic bag in the breast pocket of his shirt. "I get the best from the V.A.," he tells me, fingering the blue tablet. "They're better now than ever. They get me crazy... You know, sex isn't everything, but it has a lot to do with it. An awful lot to do with it. That's three quarters of your battle won." And it's a battle he won with Sally, even though she was the one to initiate the romance, following him home one night from poker. "She made a right turn. I asked, 'Where are you going?' She said, 'To your apartment.' And that was it."

Traditionally, nursing homes don't encourage sex. Not only do many, including Flushing House, have religious affiliations to contend with, but there's also the fact that the people footing the bill are often children and grandchildren not thrilled to imagine their forebears shacking up with someone new. Then there's the fear of sexually transmitted diseases, which, owing in part to Viagra, are famously on the rise among the geriatric population. As Al puts it, "Sex takes a little longer now, but it's wonderful for the woman. I can go on. You know?"

In response to the rising STD rate, Flushing House has invited the Visiting Nurse Service of New York to come in and lead two sex-ed programs: one for the men and one for the women. "They can't get them to talk if they do it together," Katie, the activities leader, says of her clients. "They just don't think about [STDs], because in their day and age, they didn't."

But Flushing House is an independent-living facility, not a nursing home, which drastically limits the level of supervision. Sure, the staff can stop someone from looking at porn on the communal computers, but when one resident started going out clubbing, for example, they turned a blind eye. If anything, relationships—as a useful antidote to loneliness—are encouraged. There's a darkened TV room that plays a constant cycle of romantic oldies. There are tables for two in the dining room. There are even frequent dances in the glass solarium on the roof, from where you can see all five boroughs; security cameras recently caught one couple up there going at it in the nude.

The population is overwhelmingly heterosexual—though, until recently, there was one transgender resident—and more than two thirds are female, meaning that the men typically get to do the picking. When a guy comes on the scene that the women consider a catch—someone who you can tell was handsome years ago—jostling ensues. One male resident confessed to me that he hadn't had sex in three days, as if it were a crime. Another confided that he still gets blow jobs.

The dining room is the social nexus of the facility. There's Tony and Alice's group, which is usually one of the first to be seated, with their friend Hilda begging Abraham (a staffer who escorts residents to their seats) not to put them in "Sing Sing," one of the tables farthest from the door. There's a table of five women who implore Abraham to fill the sixth seat with "either a gorgeous guy or another woman we can talk to." There's the woman who always wanted to sit with the man who looked like her dead husband, until she did and realized he wasn't like her husband at all. "I was married fifty-five and a half years," she explains. "I don't think I could go with anybody else."

The most-sought-after dinner companion of late is a man named Roosevelt, who is a young seventy-one and who wears pressed shirts and speaks in a velvety rumble. Shortly after his arrival, Abraham noticed a trend: women were trying to save a seat at their table, and as soon as Roosevelt sauntered up to the hostess stand, they would eagerly wave Abraham their way. Not that it did them much good in the end. By and large, Roosevelt feels the women at Flushing House are just too old for him.

Age, unsurprisingly, is the biggest deterrent to dating at Flushing House. Most of its residents have already nursed and lost one life partner and are not keen to do it again. As one woman explains, "I was married twice, and then I had a boyfriend. I don't want to be bothered now." Another resident tells me he doesn't want to date an older woman, but refuses to make himself "ridiculous" by being seen on the arm of a young one. Even when residents are partnered up, there can come a point when one's body becomes too fragile to entrust it to someone else. Herb and Henrietta, ninety-seven and ninety respectively, were both too sick to even come downstairs most of this past winter. "Sex?" she says. "Oh, honey, there isn't any."

Al and Sally have had the most tumultuous relationship at Flushing House. They've broken up and rekindled and broken up four or five times. Al blames Sally's declining health: not only has their sex life dropped off, but she needs a walker these days and rarely agrees to leave the building. "I want to go out," he says. "I want to drive to Jones Beach and take her to dinner. But she just says no. It wasn't like that before."

When Al's family came to visit, "I invited her all week long. I said, 'Sally, don't forget you're coming with me. We're going to eat with them. We're gonna go out to eat.' The following day, she calls me up in the morning, and she says, 'Al, I don't feel good.' I told her, 'You're full of shit.'"

Sally, for her part, can't understand why Al expects a woman her age to always be up for anything. She's had three husbands—a lifetime filled with men. If there were ever a moment when she should be let off the hook, when little should be asked of her, then that time is now.

And she isn't alone in her no-nonsense approach. The couples at Flushing House seem to engage in a distilled form of dating. There's a practicality that comes with knowing there are certain undeniable limits to how long a romance can last, or what romance at the age of eighty-five even means. Gone are certain external factors (financial viability, child-rearing capability, long-term life goals); compatibility can now boil down simply to the types of shared interests that traditionally populate personals ads—taking sunset walks or reading paperback mysteries. Couples may tell one another, as Kitty told David, "You're the best thing in my present life," but when they do pass on, they'll often be buried next to their first spouses, as if their latter-day loves never took place.

All of which takes the pressure off; no one here is burdened with finding the loves of their lives. The cafeteria's complex pecking order may recall high school, but relationships don't have nearly the same all-consuming nature as when residents were younger. Of those now dating, only Henrietta and Herb have moved in together, despite the economic advantages of double occupancy. For the most part, people don't feel the need to alter their lives substantially. "I want a little peace in my life for the first time in seventy years," Roosevelt tells me. "I want my space, and I want freedom. And I finally got it."

Bridget, a tiny woman with cherry-red hair and an Irish accent, met her ex-boyfriend Nelson a few weeks after moving into

Flushing House when they were outside the building waiting for Access-a-Ride. ("How romantic!") "I had my eye on him," she says. "He wasn't a good-looking man, but he had nice lips." Things progressed quickly from there: "Your time is limited. When you reach eighty, what have you got to lose?"

However, when Nelson left the facility to move in with family who could give him more care and asked Bridget to come with him, she was more "levelheaded." She had already been married and knew what it was like to tailor her life for a man. *Why can't it just be about having fun?*, her thinking now goes. Bridget has since become something of a flirt. She prefers to spend her time in the company of men and particularly likes one named Jim, who has so far been unresponsive, even after she tried bringing him his favorite dessert, sugar-free cookies. "He's like a stone," she says. "I can't move him."

One evening a few months ago, Flushing House's nightly poker game was shaping up to be a lively one. This is where Al fell in love with Sally. The only permanent player not in a couple was Doc, who usually deals. "Full house!" Al announced at the end of one game.

"*Ooh*, Albert, that's beautiful!" Sally proclaimed.

"Uh-huh. Can I have all that, please?" he asked, swooping a stack of dollar bills toward his end of the table and then looking over to Sally. "You're rich, sugar."

"Oh, thank you, sweetheart," she purred.

"Oh, get me a shovel!" Rita exclaimed in mock disgust. She met her husband, Irving, a World War II vet, at an upstate weekend retreat for older singles after both of their previous spouses had died. ("We like to say they ran off together," she says. "To heaven.") They married in their seventies and moved to Flushing House a few years later.

Someone asked Roosevelt, who had just joined the game, why he didn't come in to play earlier.

"I got caught on the outside with one of the residents."

"With one of the women?" asked Irving.

"Yes. She wanted to confess to me."

"Her love or what?" Rita smirked.

Roosevelt grinned back at her. "I don't want anybody hanging on my arm."

"Roosevelt, you got a line of bullshit that will sink a ship," Irving boomed, then he suddenly grew pensive. "Let me tell you something, just to be honest with you. If I didn't have Rita backing me..." He didn't complete the thought, but then he didn't need to. It was clear he relied on Rita's care, which was why their last trip to Atlantic City had been so hard. They'd been given a room with a Jacuzzi, and Irving had wanted to get in. "I wanted the two of us to go in there to see what we could do," he said, looking over at Rita. "But when it came to trying to get in, I couldn't lift my foot up high enough to get over. And if I would have gotten in, how am I going to get out?"

"That was supposed to have been a handicapped room," Rita jumped in, protectively. "It wasn't a good room." (A few months after I met Irving and Rita, Irving passed away.) Sally gripped Al's arm. Their relationship was still hot and heavy at the time. Yet when the cards were put away, they headed back to their respective rooms. No matter where they are as a couple, they've never spent the night together, though Al has wanted to on many occasions. "She has a really tremendous bed with pillows, beautiful linen. My bed, she almost fell out of! I had to hold her." But Sally values her space and her rest. From their own beds, like high-school sweethearts, they'd usually call each other from under the covers. But their conversations, as Sally recalls, were anything but sweet. "When we'd talk on the phone, I'd say, 'If anybody is listening, their ears will burn off!'"

Notes from a Unicorn
Seth Fischer

Back in 2002, when I was still in college, I lived in DC for a quarter in a quad dorm room that felt like the set of a queerish Adam Sandler movie. I—a semi-closeted bisexual drunk—lived with a gay guy from Beverly Hills I'll call Mark; James, a kind-hearted straight stoner with whom I shared a room; and Mark's best friend, an even straighter dude who looked exactly like Corey Feldman. I had a secret crush on Mark. Sometimes the four of us would stay up late at night watching CNN and drinking. For special occasions, we went to the Cheesecake Factory. Then we'd get up and be interns, whatever that meant, for the people who ran the world because that's how we thought we could go about saving it.

Mark hit on me the way gay men hit on straight men they're already comfortable with, the way straight women hit on gay men. He'd go "Mmmmm" when I walked by and say, "Why are you straight again?" He could tell it made me a little uncomfortable but not too uncomfortable. He could tell I liked it a little. He was tall and good looking and rich, and he'd tell me all about his trips giving road head to hot flight attendants in the Florida Keys. He might have been telling me the plot of a porn he'd watched or it might have been the truth, but I was enthralled and jealous and disgusted and turned on.

One night, the four of us went out together for drinks. Across from our dorms was a place called The Fox and The Hound where we smoked cigarette after cigarette. For three bucks, you could order a whiskey and Coke, which meant they'd bring you a bucket glass full of well whiskey and a tiny bottle of soda. We drank and gossiped. Mark's foot brushed my leg. I don't know if it was on purpose or if he thought it was a table leg, but I let his foot keep brushing mine, over and over, and I lost my breath for a second. He was looking at Corey Feldman, talking about some date he'd just been on. He hated straight places. "I'm bored I'm bored I'm bored," he said, jumping out of his seat, trying to talk us into going to a gay bar. Corey Feldman wasn't having it. "Fuck," I said finally, "Let's just go back up to the room."

We stumbled across the street, made it to the apartment and sat down in the living room, all of us on the couch but Mark, who was standing. He still wanted to leave. Someone plopped on CNN.

It had been eating at me. He'd been flirting with me since I moved in. I hadn't told many people, but this was different. He had to know, or if he found out later, he'd have a right to resent me. I didn't want that.

"Mark," I said, and then I mumbled at him for a bit until he rolled his eyes at me.

"Spit it out."

"You should know that I'm bi."

This was the part where in my imagination he smiled, maybe gave me a hug, and welcomed me to his club, where the streamers came from the ceiling and the music started blaring. Instead, he took a seat on a chair near the couch. His smile disappeared. Everyone was sober all of the sudden. Corey Feldman, who was sitting next to me, said something like, "That's my cue, bro," and went to bed. James stayed put, his eyes glued to the TV, but not a peep came from him, either.

I sighed and fell back farther into the couch.

Mark looked down at the ground for a minute and shook his head. He wanted to say something and stopped himself. He picked his head up and looked me right in the eyes.

"You like men *and* women?"

"Yep," I said. I hadn't told many people yet, but I'd done it enough. I knew that the questions were coming.

"I don't believe in that."

I flipped him off, smiling. "I'm sitting right here."

He recoiled a little and rubbed his hands through his hair. "No, no, sorry. What I meant is, well, do you prefer one or the other?"

His whole body was turned toward me now.

"It's just...the person. I'm attracted to the person," I said.

He stared at me. The wrong facial expression, just a little something wrong with the curl of my lips, and he would never believe me. He could mark me off as gay but not ready or just out for attention. I had to be just the right amount of angry and the right amount of confident.

He turned the TV down.

"So why aren't you out?" he asked.

"I want to work in politics," I said, enunciating now like Peter fucking Jennings. "I'm lucky enough to be attracted to women, too, you know? This business isn't easy."

He looked back at the TV, where I'm guessing something or other was blowing up on the other side of the world, and nodded.

"That's probably pretty smart," he said, a little bit of edge in his voice. I took another shot and headed off to bed. James asked me if I was okay before he headed into the shower. I said, "Sure."

Mark sat in the chair, alone now, flipping through the channels.

Two weeks after I came out to Mark, I met a woman named Kate in a course about drug policy we had to take while doing our internships. Our professor ranted every day about the evils of needle exchanges and medical pot. Anytime I disagreed, he'd say, "You must be from Santa Cruz." He was right. Both Kate and I were students at Santa Cruz, but we hadn't met until that quarter in DC. After class, I caught her eyes as she was trying to make an exit and asked, "So, do you want to hang out?" She said, "Sure," and then ran off. But I messed up and forgot to ask for her number. I never ask anyone out, but I couldn't get her out of my head. I waited for the next week, and then I got in the same elevator she did and asked for her number, in front of everyone, so she had to give it to me. Then—I'd never done this before either—I actually called her. And she said yes. She went out with me on date after date and every fucking second I was around her I wanted to be touching her, somewhere, anywhere, even just her wrist.

After a couple of dates, we went to her room. One of her roommates was always out at clubs looking for Navy guys and the other was gone. We had some drinks. I held her hand and said, "Can I kiss you?" like a fucking idiot, because I had no idea how to do this, how to be the one smitten. I kissed her cheek, then her ear, then her mouth, and she kissed back. I started shaking, my back started shaking, and I tried to figure out how to make myself stop, but I couldn't, so I just went with it. She didn't say anything, but she moaned back when I kissed her. We eventually made it to her bed, and even though she lived in a crappy dorm, too, it was the coziest place I'd ever been. She told me I smelled bad—getting used to DC's humidity wasn't easy after Santa Cruz. Instead of taking it personally and storming off or ignoring her I replaced my deodorant with antiperspirant and started putting it on every single day, which she thought was hilarious. Later, she said, "I like your smell now, but you should keep the antiperspirant on for other people's sake." I went around for about a day thinking, "She likes my nasty smell!" and dancing with myself.

A few weeks into it, I told her I was bi—the first time I'd ever told a girlfriend that—and she said, "Does that mean you'll break up with me for a guy someday?"

"No, of course not," I said.

I didn't. Instead, we broke up because I chose to take a job working for a congresswoman in Palo Alto instead of moving with her to Manhattan.

In the few years I spent working in politics pretending I wasn't bi, I learned a lot of things, but the most disturbing thing I learned was how to win: What you do is find the simplest possible message that resonates with people—and when I say simple, think, "It's the economy, Stupid" or in local races just, "Bob for State Senate"—and then you repeat it ad nauseam and get other people to repeat it ad nauseam and then ask them to get other people to repeat it until every front lawn and bulletin board and doorhanger and public space in the place you care about is filled with your message.

Somehow, in the last half century, LGBT activists have pulled off one of the biggest public relations coups in history while dealing with one of the most complex issues. It was less than forty years ago that the American Psychological Association agreed to stop saying non-straight people were sick. Today, I work at a school with a program that's created just to train therapists to be sensitive to the needs of LGBT people. Ten years ago, in *Lawrence v. Texas,* the Supreme Court stopped thirteen states from prosecuting people for sodomy; today, seventeen states allow gay marriage or domestic partnership.

All still isn't good. Besides ex-gay camps, which have destroyed countless lives, LGBT people are victims of violent hate crimes at six times the overall rate, it's legal to fire people for being gay in twenty-nine states, and being gay is illegal in seventy-six countries and punishable by execution in five. That's the short list. I could go on for pages.

But now that we've had some success, now that we have a voice and a foothold, gay rights advocates who are fighting for LGBT rights—for my rights—have to choose between two different talking points:

1) Gays and lesbians are intrinsically attracted to same-sex partners.

2) Gays and lesbians do not have a choice about being attracted to same-sex partners. It is intrinsic to who they are. While no one has a choice about their sexual orientation, sometimes, not always, bisexual people are attracted to more than one gender. So those people who are born with a more fluid sexuality can choose who they sleep with, and sometimes they may be choosing between a man and a woman, but that doesn't mean they have chosen to be attracted to both men and women.

Which talking point would you rather use?

* * *

I started jerking off when I was nine. I remember my favorite fantasy. I pictured everyone in my third-grade class, standing at their desks. Everyone took off their clothes because they got in trouble for something. It didn't matter what. My imagination zoomed in on some boy or girl. I wouldn't think about sex with them, really. My knowledge of sex at that age came from watching *Look Who's Talking*. I thought you'd kiss someone and then have a baby. I'd just think of them naked, boys and girls, and maybe I'd think of kissing them, and sometimes I'd think about their butts. I'd touch myself, and it made me feel good.

It wasn't until I'd moved in with my dad up in Boston a couple of years later that I let it hit me that anything was different. I was running the mile, in gym class, and our teacher brought us over to the high school for that because there wasn't a track at my school.

It was 1990 or 1991. My mom wanted me to look cool, but she was from L.A., not Boston, so she had me dressing like some kind of weird white preppy surfer member of N.W.A, with terrible neon-green shorts that went down to my knees and a bright orange hypercolor shirt that got brighter as I sweated on it. No one would talk to me, obviously, but I kept pace with two kids who would at least let me run near them.

One of their uncles had just died. "He was totally a fag," said the nephew. The other kid said, "But that's your uncle you're talking about." "Yeah, but he was a fag, and that's what happens to fags, with AIDS, you know?" They weren't saying it to be cruel to the uncle—there wasn't an ounce of cruelty in their voice, even though they were saying *fag*. It was just the word they knew. They used the same tone I'd heard them use when they told me the story about going into that one overgrown house where there's supposedly a hunchback inside. And it was then that it hit me, as I was jogging, even though I already knew, really, but I hadn't let myself think about it.

"Fags like boys, so I'm a fag."

That day after school I ran up straight into my room. My room had always been filthy, but I threw everything off one little section of carpet near my desk and my dresser with the trap door I would always write stories on, and I kneeled there, and said over and over to myself, "Fags like boys, so I'm a fag," crying and crying, not once thinking about that page from a magazine hidden in my desk, three feet from my head, with the naked women sprawled in impossible positions, the one I'd been beating off to every night for the last week, and not once thinking about the girl I'd kissed on the lips, my first kiss ever, a few weeks before, when my heart went pitter-patter and did all the things hearts are supposed to do during a first kiss, the girl whose heart I later broke because I thought I was a fag. I didn't want to bring her down with me because being a fag was this cancer that would grow inside me and eat up the straight part of me until I'd die of AIDS and never be able to do anything with my life.

A year later, I sat at my desk with a knife, poking at my wrist. I had an impossible crush on a boy. Frank Martin and I were on the same basketball team. His locker was two over from mine, and I couldn't help it—I was twelve or thirteen years old. I had twenty boners a day. It's just the way it was—so when he changed, I kept sneaking a peek because I just wanted to see, because I could smell him, and it was amazing, and was it too much to smell *and* see?

And he caught me looking. But when he caught me, he wouldn't look right back at me. Instead, he looked at the locker in front of him, and said, quiet enough so no one would hear, "I don't give a fuck if you're gay. I know it's not your fault, but you better not fucking look at me like that ever again."

I decided that day that I would choose to grow the part of me that liked women and kill the part that liked men. I poked at little parts of my wrist until they turned bright red, then I pulled the blade up and watched my skin turn back to its normal color, and then I pressed down again harder. But I couldn't make myself do it hard enough, because I couldn't stand blood, because I was too afraid to die right then. I tried to spell out words with the little red dots but they disappeared too quickly. I tried to spell out *Frank*. I tried to spell out *tired*. I took out a pack of stolen Kools and snuck outside and smoked cigarette after cigarette after cigarette.

Thirteen years later, right after quitting the job with the congresswoman, I was in the shower, jerking off, thinking about women—I'd mostly thought about women, really, since Frank, except for all the men—and then, out of nowhere, I thought about this guy I knew who hit on me all the time. I imagined going up to him and wrapping my arms around his huge bear chest and kissing his ear, nibbling and then blowing a bit on his neck. My breath came quick and fast, and my legs gave out, and I had to lie down in the shower and let the water pass over me, and I wasn't even jerking off anymore, it was more powerful than that. I was thinking about him and floating and it wasn't until the water got so cold I couldn't stand it that I got up and dried off and slept better than I'd slept in thirteen years.

Soon after, I came out on Myspace. There was no coming back from that.

Here's the thing I want to tell Human Rights Campaign and Equality California and all the gay rights groups who have done such incredible work, who now have their own buildings in Washington and are thinking in terms of talking points and "ramifications" and focus groups and public polling:

The gay rights movement has been so successful because activists like Harvey Milk encouraged people to come out and tell the truth to their families, to their friends and to their coworkers, to be everything they were, to say "We're here, we're queer," yes, but also, implicitly, to say, "We're here, it's complicated and probably it'd be good if we talked about this over tea."

Recently, on OKCupid, a woman messaged me: *Are you truly into ladies, and if so, what type? Finding a truly bi man is like finding a unicorn.*

If I'm a unicorn where I live now, in L.A., then I was a unicorn Rocky Mountain oyster when I moved to the old rust-belt city of Syracuse, New York, to go to grad school and live for the first time as a fully out bi man. There was one other mythical bi man in the entire city, but try as I might, I never found him. At the gay bar, I sometimes got called a "half-breeder." Straight people treated me just as shittily as they treat gay people. Three times, gay men hit me in the back of the head when they saw my head turn for a woman. For the most part, straight women wouldn't date me because, as one said, "You're just gonna leave me to go suck a dick." For the first time in my life, frat boys called me *fag*. My professor said, "The world just isn't ready for gay marriage." I emailed him "Letter from a Birmingham Jail." Then I went out with friends and my gay friends didn't know what to do because I got drunk and flirted with a lesbian. A friend said she thought bi people didn't exist. I said, "I'm sitting right here," because that was my answer, but I was starting to believe her. I stopped telling people what I was. I let people think what they wanted, which was usually that I was like them.

About a year into being there, I thought, *Why don't I just call myself gay?* I would see if I could do it before I told people, I thought. I mean, except for the occasional straight porn, and that one girl, and maybe that other one, I was only dating men. I made it a point. No more straight porn. No more thinking of women. No more dating women.

A few months later, I found myself in bed with a guy. I'd been doing well making up for lost time. No women, no women at all, except for a tiny bit of porn. I was almost ready to just say, "I'm gay. You guys were right. That bi thing was bullshit." I was getting better at the whole blow job thing. I was tied to the bed because I love being tied to the bed. I couldn't move. I moaned and screamed and made all the right noises, but then it was time, and he started to expect an end because it was getting late—dogs needed to be fed and teeth brushed and homework finished—but I just couldn't come. I just couldn't. He was getting tired and starting to look around but he didn't stop, thank god, because it would have ruined it, because I was right on the edge. Right there. So I did what no one admits to their lovers they do but that everyone does: I closed my eyes and let my mind wander to other people. I thought about men. I was sitting there forcing myself to think about men, only men, men men men men men men, and then it slipped in there, like when someone says don't think about rhubarb pie and you think about rhubarb pie. I thought, for a second, about Willow from "Buffy the Vampire Slayer," because I'd watched an episode earlier that day. Then I fucking erupted. I came so hard I was worried about getting enough air. I hope Alyson Hannigan doesn't take out a restraining order on me for admitting that, but it's important. Not because I came like that, and not because it's ridiculous, which it totally is, but because I'd tried to make a choice to be straight but it wouldn't work and now I'd tried to be gay and it wouldn't work.

I wanted to join a team so I wouldn't have to answer any more questions, so I wouldn't have to say that I preferred one or the other or whether I exist or if I'm a unicorn or how I can ever hope to be monogamous if I'm attracted to more than one gender. But I failed to choose a side, so now, for once, I'm going to answer all of these questions honestly:

I don't know. I can't speak for other bi people, but only for myself. I just don't know.

I don't know because I can't get all the voices out of my head, the ones that ask all the wrong questions. The ones that tell me I must be one thing or the other—for whom, or why, I don't know. The voices want a neat fit, but I can't accommodate them. I've tried, and I can't, and I shouldn't.

No one will ever make this go away. No one will ever make it simple.

And maybe, just maybe, that's how I win.

Rest Stop Confidential
Conner Habib

I was fifteen the first time I found out that men have sex in public. On the way to Maine with my mom and stepfather, we pulled off the highway and into a rest area. At the urinal, there was a man next to me. He was tall and homely, and holding himself. He stared at me. I was electrified, but held to that spot; he shook himself at me and I couldn't move. We would have stayed there forever, but another man came in and saw what was happening and scowled. Time started again and I ran out of the bathroom.

If you've ever pulled over to a rest area, you've been near men having sex. I'm one of those men, I've done it a hundred times; we go into the woods or a truck with tinted windows, in a stall under cold light. It never stops, not for season or time. In the winter, men trudge through snow to be with each other, in the summer, men leave the woods with ticks clinging to their legs. Have you ever stopped at a rest area and found it completely empty? There's always one man there, in his car, waiting to meet someone new.

This has been going on for a long, long time. The new ways that men meet—endlessly staring into phones, searching on hookup apps like Grindr or sites like Manhunt—haven't changed the fact that we're still having sex at rest areas, because they offer something different. For the man who is unsure of his sexuality, or unsure of how to tell others about it, for the man who has a family but feels new desires (or old, hidden ones) unfolding inside of him, the website and the phone apps are just too certain of themselves. They're for gay men who want to have gay sex. Sex at the rest area, instead, abolishes identity; there's a sort of freedom there to not be anything—instead, men just meet other men there; men who want the same sort of freedom.

Is it any wonder why people who feel the weight of their identities have been caught having sex at rest areas? Sen. Larry Craig and pop star George Michael were both discovered having sex at them. There is an appeal not just to having sex, but to having anonymous sex—not because you want to hide your identity from the other person; surely the other men recognized George Michael—but to feeling your own identity left behind. And this freedom is open to everyone, even those comfortable with their sexuality.

When I was twenty-one, on the day I got my first car, I drove to a little parking lot off the highway near where I lived: the gravity of memory—of that day when I was fifteen—drew me there. Later, on the long drives between college in Massachusetts and home in Pennsylvania, I'd pull over whenever I found a rest stop. When I got there, I would wait. I wasn't nervous, I wasn't thinking—it seemed like where I should be.

Sometimes men go to rest areas because there's nowhere else to go. My college town and my hometown were surrounded by thick lines of trees and post-industrial abandoned factories. There was no way to meet anyone, or if there was, it felt forced, somehow. Maybe I could go on dates with a few guys who were out like me, but I didn't really want to go on dates, so it would've been dishonest. The straight students were going to parties and hooking up, making out on the green, having sex in dorms. The gay guys had to do what they could, wherever they could find it. Making out drunkenly with straight also-drunk frat boys, sex in the library with townies, trips to the nearest big city: either do those things or sit with your sexual feelings, like many of us had our entire lives. All that energy and nowhere to put it, no one to share it with.

Someone else would park next to me and look over. There were lots of old men, and younger ones too. There was no signal, just the way we looked at one another. We could tell. I would go into the little bathroom building, like the one in Maine. At the urinals, when the bathroom was mostly empty, we could stand side by side and reach over to each other. Or if not at the urinals, someone would be sitting in the stall next to me, tapping his foot, and I'd get on the cold dirty floor and slide my body halfway underneath the divider or sometimes there'd be a hole in the wall.

After a while I began to develop a strange feeling at rest areas, like I was giving myself to someone. Not that I gave my full self, but that the part of myself I did give was complete. There was no pretense, no awkward conversation or dancing around whether or not I should be attracted to somebody. There was no wondering if someone was straight or gay; there was no sexual orientation at all. We were just there, together, as ourselves.

Often, there was fence that blocked off the woods, and a break in that fence cut by someone who had been there before. There was a path of mud through the grass, worn down by use.

In the woods, we'd find a clearing, and there, many things would happen. So many people and bodies, all looking for the same thing. So many of us past the fence, in the woods, under the sky. It was easy, at times like that, to see that there are far more men in need of other men than anyone knows.

And just as people's identities blurred up, so did the idea of place itself; that was part of the appeal. Once I saw a bag of condoms nailed to a tree with a sign that read, BE SAFE GUYS. It was a kind gesture, but it somehow felt like an intrusion. Because these places weren't quite places, they weren't destinations; not for most people. They were away from hookup websites; away from houses, bars, clubs, lives—removed from the world. And when the world crept in, it made the experience less real, less itself.

Intrusions came in other forms, too. The police pulled into a rest area I was at in Rhode Island once. It was night. I calmly leaned my car seat back and pretended to be sleeping. They shined a light in and I rolled down the window.

"What are you doing out here," one asked.

"Just resting," I said.

They looked at each other. "All right. Well, you know, a lot of guys come here for fun and games."

"Fun and games?"

"Yeah."

"What, like drugs?" I asked, playing stupid.

They couldn't say it. They couldn't say anything. They told me to take care and drove off.

The police are a constant threat to rest area sex—they want so badly to blend the world into it.

That's the opposite of why people go. Some of the men at rest areas are stepping out of their lives. They're not simply escaping their marriages, or their parents or their circumstances; at rest areas, they're allowing themselves to be honest.

Once, after hooking up with a man in a stall, we walked out into the calm day together. I saw him go to his car, a car I hadn't noticed before. In it, his children were waiting for him. Who knows what his life was like outside that stall?

His children were young and excited, crawling over each other in the backseat. He opened their door and said something to them I couldn't hear. They calmed down and buckled up. I leaned against my car, with nowhere to be, and he got in his and drove away and did not look back.

It's not "fun and games." It's men yielding to something they might be trying to deny, but can't. These places give wholly different lives to some people. I don't know if these men are "gay" or "straight." Does it matter? At a spot that for most people is on the way to somewhere else, men can meet each other and meet themselves.

I live in San Francisco now, and there's more acceptance here of sexuality and identity than anywhere I've ever been. There's also very little anonymous sex. "Anonymous" sex here means meeting a man online or on Grindr or at the bar, learning his name, going back to his apartment or mine. It's not a bad thing, of course, but I miss being a nobody at an in-between place, a no-place. Here, I have to be somebody, everything is so defined around the edges. At the rest area, I could just be a body, be there for some other body that I didn't know, that was longing for the sort of comfort and love that only no one, nowhere could give.

When on Fire Island...
A Polyamorous Disaster
Nicholas Garnett

My wife, Rachael, and I stood by a Jacuzzi on Fire Island with a dozen gay men. We were all watching Jason have at Mandy. Again. It was sex, but it wasn't particularly sexy—more Animal Planet than Spice Channel. Mandy had braced herself against the edge of the blue fiberglass tub, her ropy black hair spilling down in front of her. And with each of Jason's thrusts, a swell of water cascaded over the lip of the tub to the deck below. The sound of water slapping wood blended with the couple's moans in an oddly syncopated rhythm. It was a pretty slick groove, actually—somewhere between bossa nova and Barry White.

The men gathered around were rapt. Who could blame them? This was at least as good as any porn movie. *And* it involved a real man with huge muscles and tattoos. But Rachael sighed and walked by me in a huff, slid open the screen door leading to the living room and shut it loudly behind her. A sinking feeling pierced the haze of my high. Jason and Mandy showed no signs of letting up, so I headed inside to find Rachael.

It was Rachael who had opened the door to this world. Before I met her, I'd been floating through life, brooding, adrift, like the down-on-his-luck male lead in a film noir, nursing his drink in some saloon, wondering what was next. But Rachael was beautiful, smart and driven. So were her friends—witty, confident gay men who reveled in their success and flaunted it with cool cars, beautiful clothes and impeccably decorated homes. Rachael loved them, and so did I.

It was the mid-'90s, the era of Clinton, boom times and surplus. Over cocktails and cocaine, there was talk of Human Rights Coalition fundraisers, hot tech investments, the cost of kitchen renovations, vacations to Tuscany, and second homes in Rehoboth. In this world, Rachael and I were the exotic ones— the hot straight couple who partied like rock stars with the boys. There were group vacations to Provence, Cancun and Istanbul. There were parties in Miami, New York, Amsterdam, Montreal, Mykonos and San Francisco. We became a major subculture's minor celebrities.

In one important aspect, though, we remained outsiders. Most of our gay friends, even the ones in committed relationships, were having sex like it was the last days of the Roman Empire and they were Caligula. We heard about threeways, fourways, orgies, sex parties at home, sex in sex clubs, sex in cabs on the way back from sex clubs, sex in public bathrooms and in truck stops.

Rachael and I were curious. Everything else about this lifestyle seemed to be working for us. Could promiscuity? Not according to our best friend, Christian.

"I'm telling you," he said, "you're asking for trouble."

"You manage just fine," Rachael said. Christian and his male

partner of nearly fifteen years had avoided the emotional mine-
fields of playing the field by employing a policy of full participa-
tion when they were together and discretion when they were not.
It was an arrangement I referred to as "don't ask, don't smell."

"It is different when it's boys," Christian said. "Most of us have
a knack for separating our heads from our penises. My advice:
Treat it like live porn. Or a yoga class with a happy ending. Keep
your emotions out of it. Set some ground rules and talk about
them *before* you go there."

"Damn," I said. "Should I be writing all this down?"

Christian patted my cheek. "Laugh now, but you're getting
privileged information here. Hard-earned, too. Truth is, straight
or gay, it's a crapshoot. Everything's going along fine, then
someone sticks his willy somewhere and the damn thing blows
up like an exploding cigar."

Still, we were determined to find out for ourselves. The opportunity to do just that came in the form of Jason and Mandy,
two personal trainers we met at a club during gay pride celebra-
tions in Boston. Jason was straight; Mandy was bisexual. Most of
Jason and Mandy's clients were gay, as were many of their friends.
It seemed so perfect.

Then came Fire Island.

Narrow boardwalks wound through pine forests and connected
the houses together like the yellow brick road. Trees reverberated
with the *clickity-clack* of big men pulling little red wagons full of
groceries and luggage to and from the ferry terminal. There were
miles of desolate sand dunes and achingly beautiful sea grass–
lined beaches. Then, shoved into this bucolic utopia were New
York City sensibilities, as over the top as William Shatner re-
citing Shakespeare: designer-decorated homes where a summer
share cost the same as a three-bedroom rambler in most parts of

the country; huge, lavish parties; smaller, yet more lavish parties; social climbing galore; one-upsmanship; balls-to-the-wall, 24/7.

The only nightclub, the Pavilion, was a wooden sweatbox. In the morning, a stream of clubbed-out zombies shuffled shamelessly along the walkways looking for an after-party and sex.

The owner of the house in which we stayed was Ramon, also known as the cha-cha-doctor of Chelsea, who specialized, ironically, in the research and treatment of AIDS. (Though Ramon was not really his name. I've changed all the names in this piece, for what I assume are obvious reasons.) He was the perfect host. Anything you wanted—as long as what you wanted was sex or drugs. There were vials of everything, everywhere, all the time. If it wasn't in front of you, all you had to do was ask: K, G, X, poppers, weed, Viagra, crystal—especially crystal. Snorted, smoked or shot up, only crystal could keep the party, and the sex, going full-tilt for days.

The first people we met were the Porn Boys, feature acts in a series of videos. We nicknamed them Tweaked and Chipper. I kept forgetting their real names. This was awkward considering how often I ran into them traipsing around the house naked. The first time I walked by the Porn Boys' room with the door open, I saw what looked like a naked rugby scrum. Based on what I heard, it was a high-scoring game.

Rachael and I saw the last translucent veil separating us from our friends ripped away. We hung a welcome sign on our bed. Jason and Mandy jumped right in. High as I was, the sex had a dreamy quality, as though I was watching myself perform pornography through a Vaseline-coated camera lens.

Then, just as Christian predicted, things came undone. I happened upon Rachael and Jason having sex in the poolside shower. I tried to ignore the stab of jealousy and resentment. But

I couldn't. Mandy, jacked up on nearly everything, woke me up in the middle of the night to see the stars. We jumped in the pool and had sex as the sun came up. Mandy's sex with Jason was raw, animal-like, but with me she was tender and sweet, a perfect counterpoint to her rock-hard body.

I fell into a crush. And that's when, with the two of us standing in the shallow end of the pool, her legs wrapped around my waist, she made a confession:

"You know, I think I'm a little gaga."

My heart raced. "That makes two of us," I said.

"It's not just his looks. I've dated plenty of guys built like him—you know other trainers and bodybuilders."

Oh.

"I see," I said.

"He's so good to me. A genuinely nice guy. Slide back a little." I did. She swiveled her hips and lowered herself onto me. "There," she said, "that's better."

"Does he know?"

"Oh, he knows, all right. But I just can't get him to make a commitment. At least not the way I want him to." Her thigh muscles pulsed against my hips.

"So, you'd be willing to be exclusive if he agreed?"

"Sure. I'd be monogamous in a heartbeat with him—and with you and Rachael, of course. Pull my hair. Harder."

In the midst of having sex with an acquaintance, Mandy was proposing a monogamous relationship involving four people: two couples—one of them married—living in different cities, a union composed of two heterosexual men and a couple of bisexual women.

Then, things got really complicated.

Rachael, Ramon and I walked into the guest bedroom and

found Mandy pancaked between Jason and Ramon's boyfriend. Ramon played it off as though it didn't bother him. Rachael was mortified that our guests had appropriated our host's partner. It did strike me as bad form.

The next evening, we all went over to the neighbor's pool to watch the sunset. Rachael and I left Jason and Mandy, who gave in to the urging of the crowd and had sex on a lounge chair. The applause carried all the way over to Ramon's house.

Jason and Mandy had become the show. My crush had been crushed. Rachael's anger was smoldering. Behind my hurt feelings and Rachael's indignation hid another emotion. We were jealous—and not just of each other. We were used to being *the* hot straight couple in this scene. After having the spotlight for so long, neither of us was okay with second billing.

What followed next was a naked version of a comedy of manners—minus the comedy and the manners. Rachael confronted Mandy in the kitchen. Mandy burst into tears. Jason confronted Rachael in the bedroom about confronting Mandy. Rachael burst into tears. I confronted Jason in the living room about confronting Rachael. Rachael and Mandy burst into tears. When I confronted Rachael about cavorting with Jason, things got personal.

"You've got nerve," she said. "After that late-night stargazing session in the pool?"

"Why don't you go and snort up a few more lines," I said. "It brings out such a lovely side of you."

Our experiment had gone haywire. Someone in charge needed to pull the plug. The problem was that no one was in charge of anything.

Jason and Mandy began staging special command performances in various venues, including the living room, the pool deck, the second floor balcony, the outdoor shower, the kitchen, and most recently, the Jacuzzi, where Rachael had just left me—high and dry.

I turned the corner into one of the guest rooms. There was Rachael sitting on the bed with the Porn Boys. She was just about to inhale white smoke from the end of a small, glass water pipe. Privately, Rachael had been deriding the Porn Boys for smoking crystal, which she said hit too close to the utterly un-fabulous act of smoking crack. I had to admit, the distinction was lost on me.

Rachael saw me, lowered the pipe a few inches and shrugged. "When on Fire Island..." I sat on the edge of the bed in the Porn Boys' bedroom and watched Rachael press the glass pipe to her lips.

Except for the muffled moans coming from the hot tub, the hiss from the small butane lighter was the only sound in the room. A thin tendril of smoke streamed into Rachael's mouth.

Tweaked said, "Hold it in." Rachael puffed up her cheeks and waited. "*Now*," he said. She exhaled a small plume, like breath on a frosty morning.

Chipper pointed the pipe in my direction. "You want?"

"Yes, he does," said Rachael.

"I do?"

Rachael said, "If this is the highway to hell, I'm not riding it alone."

I tried to think of a reason not to. A good reason wouldn't be good enough. Not here. Especially not here.

Tweaked snapped on the lighter and maneuvered the pale blue flame under the crystal. It melted and was transformed from powder into a white haze.

"Draw," he said. "Not too hard."

I touched my lips to the tip of the warm glass, inhaled and watched the smoke disappear until it emerged again as a frail, white wisp. There was only the slightest chemically tinged aftertaste. A wave spread through me, euphoric, but much more. There was clarity—perfect, doubt-obliterating clarity.

From outside, Mandy's voice spiraled up, signaling her orgasm. I looked up to the ceiling. The image there was as plain as it was unambiguous: it was me and Rachael, sharing the first car on our fantasy roller coaster—a ride with no rules or limits, our arms held over our heads as it came right off the rails.

Rachael came up to me. She placed her arm on my shoulder. "You okay?"

I took a deep breath. "I think it's time to go back."

"Back?" said Chipper. "You can't go back. Not now."

Chipper was right. Rachael and I returned home, where our sleep-and-food-deprived bodies finally teamed up with our ravaged nervous systems and our bruised egos to let us have it, right in the old cerebellum. The whole damn country seemed to join us in a spectacular crash, as markets collapsed and planes smashed into buildings. Some of our friends ended up sick, others in rehab. It had been one hell of a party, but the party was over.

And so were Rachael and I. After Fire Island, a black shroud descended over us. We burrowed down into a grinding disillusionment and mutual resentment from which our relationship never really recovered. There was an affair—mine—followed by divorce.

"More is more," Rachael used to say. Maybe so. But on Fire Island I learned that, sometimes, more is just too much.

Cherry Picking
Julia Serano

The first time I learned about sex was in fifth grade. It wasn't by way of a sex education class or a Mom and Dad birds-and-the-bees speech, but rather a joke. A completely unfunny dirty joke little kids tell to pass along important information. I think the punch line was, "Mommy, Mommy, turn on your headlights! Daddy's snake is about to go into your cave!" Now, granted before hearing the joke I already had a strange relationship with my penis. I used to draw pictures of myself naked with a needle going into my penis, imagining that it contained special medicine that would make the thing disappear. Every time I used the urinal in the little boy's room, I had a sneaking suspicion something wasn't quite right. That night, after hearing the joke, I remember looking down at my penis, knowing what it was supposedly for, and I felt absolutely detached and dumbfounded.

The first time I dressed as a girl was in sixth grade. I had insomnia and one night I felt compelled to wrap a pair of white lacy curtains around my body. I stared at my reflection in the bedroom mirror for hours. I looked like a girl. Perhaps it should have been no surprise. I was prepubescent and had one of those longish, late '70s, boy haircuts. But it completely blew my mind. The scariest part about this revelation was that it somehow made perfect sense.

The first time I had a crush on someone was in seventh grade. Her name was Kathy and I thought she was cute. Nancy Phillips told me that Kathy liked me but I was too chickenshit to ask her out. So I fantasized about her instead. I imagined some bad guy had captured us both and as part of his evil scheme he would offer me two choices: he would either kill Kathy or turn me into a girl. He left it up to me to decide and I would always gallantly choose the latter. Kathy would be so impressed that I had sacrificed my maleness to save her life that she would ask me out on a date. I always said yes, and the rest of the fantasy involved different permutations of the two of us sucking face. All of this happened before I ever heard the word *lesbian*.

The first time I decided to change my sex was in tenth grade. It happened at my baseball league all-star game. I wasn't playing in the game but I went with a few friends who also didn't make the team. While we were sitting in the bleachers, a group of neighborhood girls walked by and some of my flirtier guy friends started teasing them in that teenage-boy "I like you" sort of way. Both groups struck up a conversation but I just sort of sat there and stared. It seemed so obvious to me that I should be one of those girls rather than one of these boys. It was so sad because nobody could see it but me. So I decided to get a sex-change operation. I didn't really know what it was or what it involved; I had only heard about it on TV. Later I realized if I was to pursue such a thing I would have to let all of my friends and family know I wanted to be a girl, and I couldn't think of anything more frightening. So, instead, I tucked the memory of my all-star game epiphany into the dark recesses of my brain. Like a time capsule, it wouldn't surface again for another fifteen years.

The first time I had a girlfriend was in twelfth grade. She was smart and quirky and interesting and cute and completely kick-ass. I totally fell for her; she was my first true love. After dates, we would park on a quiet, dark street and make out. Her lips were the first ones I ever kissed, her breasts the first I felt up, her vagina the first I fingered. She was one year younger than me but way more mature. When I left to go to college, she suggested we see other people. I was devastated but she said that we were both still really young and had our whole lives ahead of us. She was right.

My first supposed sexual peak came when I was eighteen. It was my first year of college and I didn't really have any freshman sexual experiences to speak of. Some years are just like that but don't feel bad for me, I made up for it by having a second sexual peak as a woman at the age of thirty-five.

The first time that I masturbated to orgasm was when I was nineteen. Nobody ever believes that it happened so late but it's true. Before then, when I'd play with myself, I would push down on my penis and rock my hand back and forth. I've been told that that's how a lot of girls do it. I just did it that way instinctually. It felt really good, but I never orgasmed. Then my college girlfriend gave me my first hand job and I learned the power of the stroke. Granted, I knew about the stroke from watching porn but it never occurred to me to try it out on myself. It worked like a charm. It's amazing how you can have a body all of your life yet there's always something new that you can learn about it. Strangely enough, I don't really remember the first time that I had penetrative sex, the supposedly landmark day when my virginity was officially lost. It's true. I know it happened when I was nineteen with the girlfriend I had throughout most of college. I've lost the particular night we popped each other's cherries in a blur of dorm-room sex scenes the two of us shared over a three-year period. Eventually she went on the pill, and since we were each other's first, we stopped using condoms. I could never get over how amazing it felt to be inside her, to feel my genitals inside her genitals. To this day, the feeling is the only part about being physically male that I fondly reminisce about.

The first time that I ever went out in public dressed as a woman was when I was twenty-one. I came home from college for Easter weekend while the rest of my family was away on a trip. I shaved off the silly-looking beard I had grown over the semester. I put on my sister's black cotton knit dress. It had long sleeves so no one could see my arm hair and I wore opaque tights to hide my leg hair. I'm sure I put way too much makeup on my face and way too much product in my hair but nobody seemed to care because it was the '80s. I drove to a mall about an hour away from my parents' house so I wouldn't run into anyone who knew me. As I approached the entrance, an older man held the door open for me and called me "sweetie," and I felt flattered and insulted at the same time but mostly I was just amazed to be getting away with it. After walking around the mall for about ten minutes, I realized I was hungry and hadn't eaten all morning so I drove to a Burger King for a shake and fries. The woman at the drive-thru window said, "Thank you, ma'am," as she handed me my change and receipt. I can't begin to tell you how beautiful those three simple words sounded.

The first time I told someone that I cross-dressed was when I was twenty-three. He was a friend of a friend and we were hanging out at a party. Out of the blue, he told me he was bisexual and he thought I was cute. I told him that I wasn't into boys but I did like dressing up as a girl. We talked about it all for a couple of hours. When I woke up the following morning, I practically died of embarrassment.

The first time I kissed a boy was when I was twenty-four. It happened in the Bronx. I was coming to terms with my submissive fantasies and met a dominant guy through a personal ad he had placed in the *Village Voice*. In my fantasies I was always female but I was afraid to go to his place cross-dressed, so instead I went in drab (tranny talk for "dressed as a boy"). When I got there, he was dressed head-to-toe in leather and reeked of patchouli. His stereo was blasting Depeche Mode, which seemed really cliché. He tied me to his bed, blindfolded me and began kissing and groping me. It was extra-weird because he had a moustache and I kept imagining that his mouth was some strange combination of a porcupine and a leech. It wasn't a lot of fun. I'm sure he didn't enjoy himself much either, what with me being a confused and inexperienced bottom who just sort of lay there doing nothing. Afterward, we both talked about our favorite Woody Allen films. I never saw him again.

The first time I had sex with someone while in femme mode was when I was twenty-eight. She was a bisexual friend who I dated on and off for a bit. First we went to the SF MoMA to see a Frida Kahlo exhibit. Then we went back to her place and shared a bottle of wine. We kissed. She fondled my foam breast through my shirt and told me how much she missed being with a woman. She lent me some clothes that were less dorky than the ones I had on, and she took it upon herself to redo my makeup and hair. She made me look way better than I did earlier that day. We left her house to go to the Chameleon, a local dive bar. She laughed when the Latino boys in her neighborhood made the snake sounds at me. We had a few beers and talked.

It was like two girls talking, she even said so. We both cried at one point. I'm not exactly sure why but in retrospect I think it was because we both realized how sad it was that I had to keep this part of me hidden most of the time. Afterward we went back to her place and had sloppy sex. She wanted me to penetrate her but I couldn't keep it up. How could I after all of that? The next morning, I woke up and realized I didn't bring any boy clothes along because I wasn't planning on spending the night. She lent me a pair of her pants and a hockey jersey to wear on the return trip to my apartment. She was a lot bigger than me so when I put on the shirt it felt like I was wearing a tent. I seemed so small. I can't remember ever feeling less like a boy than I did sitting on the DART train wearing that hockey jersey.

I met Dani, who would eventually become my wife, when I was thirty. We shared lots of firsts together. She was the first dyke activist that I ever dated, the first person I ever moved in with, the first person I shared a checking account with. We even merged our CD collections. She was the first person to take me with a strap-on dildo, the first to give me a purely anal orgasm, the first person who truly understood how to make love to my physically male body while relating to me as a woman. Dani was by my side the day I first called myself "queer" and the day I first dared to refer to myself as "transgendered." She was the first and only person I ever asked to marry me. On a rainy night, during the brief period when we were calling each other "fiancée," the two of us were lying in our bed. I told her I was thinking about transitioning. We held hands and talked about it through the night. In the morning she took me out to breakfast by Lake Merritt. She made me laugh. Somehow she made the scariest day of my life really, really beautiful.

The first time I took female hormones was when I was thirty-three. It was the day after our honeymoon. I washed the pills down with water, then sat on the balcony of our apartment waiting for the buzz to hit.

The first time I had a female orgasm was about two months after that. I was masturbating, and for the first time in my life the stroke just wasn't doing it. I just needed…more. So I grabbed Dani's Hitachi Magic Wand. A few years back I had tried out her vibrators but they were way too much stimulation for my male orgasm. But now, after two months of being on female hormones, I could place her vibrator directly onto the tip of my penis and… wow! Suddenly I found myself writhing for ten or fifteen minutes straight, in a sexual state at least twenty times more intense than any boy orgasm I had ever had. I decided right there and then I was never going back.

The first day I lived as a woman was a day that Dani and I had planned to celebrate. On our honeymoon, she bought an expensive bottle of wine for us to share on that special occasion. However, some firsts don't happen in a very clear-cut fashion. There was no first day of being female for me. Instead, I just gradually changed over a five-month period and before I knew it, strangers were referring to me as "she" even though I was still dressing in drab. We ended up drinking that bottle of wine on our wedding anniversary instead.

Some people have asked if I will become a virgin again when I eventually have bottom surgery. You know, a vaginal virgin of sorts. I just laugh. The whole idea of virginity is utterly ridiculous, as if every person's life can be divided up neatly into an innocent childlike half and the impure adult half. People who believe this must have excruciatingly boring and simplistic sex lives.

For me, there have been many first times and each has given

me a rare opportunity to see myself a bit differently. My life has no singular defining point because each first time is dependent upon all of the other ones that came previously. And while having surgery may mark the end of my physical transition to female, I don't see my sexual evolution as reaching some sort of conclusion. If there is one thing I've learned, it's that there will always be more first times to look forward to in my future.

Holy Fuck: The Fourth-and-Long Virgin
Jon Pressick

It all started at one press conference. Amongst a throng of journalists, one voice rang out. One voice asked a seemingly out of place question. One voice asked Tim Tebow if he was a virgin. And when he said, "Yes," a monster was let loose. Or rather, a monster remains confined.

The mythic status of Tebow's lack of sex is as legendary as his football career. Yes, he's a virgin. Yes, he has strong religious convictions and he wants to wait for the "right woman." Really, there isn't that much to the story. Same as his actual career. Yes, he's a football player. Yes, he's waiting for the perfect marriage of potential and skill. But Tim Tebow is a professional athlete and that just isn't the way pro ball players are supposed to act. They're supposed to be pro ballers! In recent times we have Shawn Kemp, basketball player and father to seven children with six different women. We have Tiger Woods with his cross-country exploits and affinity for diner waitresses. They got to where they are (the beds, hotels, backseats of the nation) because they are allowed—and encouraged—to. Their stature as athletes affords them this sexual stature.

But of course, all athletes looking to score must admire the legendary dedication to his craft that Wilt "The Stilt" Chamberlain demonstrated over the course of his illustrious career. And the man had time to play basketball too! The estimate is that Chamberlain had over twenty thousand sexual partners in his lifetime. When he gets to it, Tebow is going to have a lot of catching up to do. But the thing is, he doesn't want to go for that gold. He wants one woman. He wants to be in love. He wants a life partner. And for this he is reviled and mocked in mainstream media.

The accepted norm for athletes—male athletes—is that they are to be unstoppable on the field of play *and* in playing the field. They are to be virile, masculine and ready to fuck anything that moves. Athletes are adored and respected for their bodies, and how they use them. Their inflated strength, endurance and testosterone are supposed to carry over from their sporting activity to the rest of their lives. They conquer. They vanquish. The ancient Greeks would sculpt rock into beautiful art to reflect the admiration of athletic bodies. Now young children hang posters on their walls of their favorite players.

But this is not all projection from the outside in. Athletes do not just become sexual gods because we tell them to. In his essay "The Myth of the Sexual Athlete," Dr. Don Sabo argues much of the bravado and confidence needed to become high scorers is learned by young athletes in dressing rooms with their peers.[1] As boys learn to compete against other boys in sporting arenas, they also learn to compete in sexual matters. Locker room talk is the norm and sharing details of getting-in-her-pants escapades is expected. So, according to Sabo, this can lead to men growing up detached from the idea of sexual and emotional commitment. Without that feeling, it becomes far easier to see why so many athletes live by the Five Finger Rule (any port in a storm). It would seem that Tim Tebow must have been too busy listening to hymns or sermons or Christian rock on his iPod to catch this part of team bonding.

Much has been said of Tebow's strong religious beliefs and usually it is Tebow himself doing the talking. Here's where the issue with mainstream culture comes into play. If Tebow were just a football player leading a quiet, pious life, not getting any and happy that way, no one would care. But when you paint Bible verses on your face and talk about your faith all the bloody time, people perk up and take notice. Sure, he's trying to continue his family's life of missionary work, but his talking about his lonely jockstrap rubs people the wrong way.

Funny thing is, Tebow is no trailblazer. Heard of A.C. Green? He is predominantly remembered as a supporting member of those dominant Los Angeles Lakers teams of the 1980s. He got around and played for a few other teams before winding down his career and retiring in 2001. He won three championships and holds the record for most consecutive games played. He was also a vocal virgin throughout his entire career.

In a 1998 essay in *Ebony*[2], the deeply religious Green revealed that teammates tried to tempt him, but he always refused. Instead he tried to convince them of the dangers of their ways. He also railed against the promiscuous culture in the NBA:

> I tell my colleagues and teammates all the time that they are playing with fire. They don't realize how stupid it is because to them it's fun, it's daring, it is like

living on the edge. And when you live on the edge, you want to be near the fire. But like mama said, when you play with fire, you might get burned. These guys have so much to lose. It's crazy to me to put yourself in that position. There might be a few virgins in the NBA. But overall, the guys are sort of reckless and their behavior reflects the attitude, "Hey, I can do anything and everything and not worry about responsibility and accountability." That's their attitude.

Sometimes in the locker room, I'm like a voice of reason. I don't want to hear about what happened last night, and the guys have enough respect for me and know what I stand for that they don't even bring that stuff to me. But more than anything I try to get them to understand that you've got to think about what you're doing—instead of just thinking that every lady out there is a road trip. That's the type of mentality sometimes—"just because I go from city to city and play this game, I can play women too." Sometimes they think women are just like that—a game or a piece of meat.[3]

Green got married in 2002, after his playing days ended.

Will the same good fortune happen for Tim Tebow? If it takes his entire career, will he be able to hold out for Mrs. Right instead of Ms. Right Now?

That is the big question now that he's off to play in New York City. If he actually were inconspicuous, then maybe he'd be able to get by better. But he's the missionary who never stops proselytizing. And he's heading to the city that never sleeps, where the denizens want to know who celebrities are sleeping with.

Not that we haven't been wondering who makes Tebow's jock itch already. He is a very pretty man. He's got the body; he's got the looks. Combine those factors with a fervent Christian belief and he must be gay, right? Okay, so those ideas don't really seem to go together, but more and more rumors are flying that Tim Tebow is actually a deeply closeted, self-loathing queer. Seems a stretch, but the pervasive idea is that other deeply religious Christian zealots (Ted Haggard, John Paulk) were actually canoodling with cock while maintaining firm antigay stances. Flamer flames were certainly fueled by the Tim and Tom Brady Manhunt Mobile parody ad. And despite his strong Christian convictions (including appearing in an antiabortion ad run during the Super Bowl), Tebow has not come out with any definitive statements about the LGBT community.

So, could he be? There is strong sentiment that if Tebow ever does do a backfield rush out of the closet, he could be a tremendous bridge-building figure. Maybe he could get the Christians and the gays together. Maybe he could be *the* common ground. He would certainly be one of the most high-profile Christians to embrace his queer identity. Hell, he'd probably do better with them than he would the rest of his NFL fraternity.

When it comes to tackling Tim Tebow though, no one is more interested in getting Tim's pants down than Noel Biderman, but the CEO of AshleyMadison.com, the world's premier dating site for people who want to cheat on their partners, isn't interested in Tebow in a gay way. No, he's taken things to a whole new level by putting a bounty on Tebow's virginity. With an offer of one million dollars on the table, Biderman is looking for anyone who can provide proof that Tebow is not a virgin after all. Or anymore. A statement from the website affirms the notion that sports and sex are synonymous: "Sports and sex (and of course, infidelity) go hand in hand. If Mr. Tebow is indeed abstaining from adult relationships, I would encourage him to find a nice lady or two and enjoy his youth and fame as much as possible."[4] Just imagine what would happen if he were to claim that check.

So it looks like everyone else is looking to get Tim Tebow laid...except Tim Tebow. Why doesn't he fit into our neat little box for athletes? Why don't we let him live his life in virginal peace? When did remaining a virgin become unnatural? Should Tim listen to Noel Biderman and the queer community, hunker down and lay some pipe—whichever line is available?

No. He should keep on doing what he's doing. So much work, so much activism, so many lives have gone into creating sex-positive culture that we cannot undo all of that by being hypocrites. And telling Tim Tebow he shouldn't be a virgin, he shouldn't wait until marriage, and he shouldn't have religious beliefs creates a sex-negative situation for him. Nobody is telling him to fuck because he wants to and it feels nice. No, Tim Tebow is being told to fuck because he's *supposed* to want that. In doing so, we're giving everyone the right to tell other people "You shouldn't be a slut," "You shouldn't have sex before marriage," "You should wait for the right person." Granted, it would be great if Tebow would keep his mouth as still as his penis is. However, he needs to be respected as a sexual man who has beliefs. And when that lucky person comes along for Tim Tebow, here's hoping she or he has a strong defense, because he's going to be coming with a Hail Mary.

Notes

1   D. Sabo. (1999). "The Myth of the Sexual Athlete." Reprinted in Estelle Disch, editor, Reconstructing Gender: A Multicultural Anthology (London: Mayfield Publishing Company, 2002).

2   A.C. Green "Male virgin NBA star A.C. Green tells 'Why I have refused sex'". Ebony. FindArticles.com. 03 May, 2012.

3   Ibid.

4   Ashley Madison, (2012). Untitled [Press release]. Retrieved from http://news.ashleymadison.com/2012/04/24/news/sports/ashley-madison-puts-1-million-bounty-on-tim-tebows-virginity.

Baby Talk
Rachel Kramer Bussel

"I want to be a good boy for my mommy," said the man. He was in his forties, and he was naked in bed with me. I guess this wasn't your typical second date.

It wasn't the first time the *M* word had been mentioned in our dirty talk, either. But when it came up on the phone, I could just laugh it off or pretend I hadn't heard him. Not this time. Now, it was real. He wanted me to pretend to be his mommy—his naughty, flirtatious, sexy mommy. Even for a professional sex writer like me, with nineteen years of adventures behind her, "age play" was out there.

A subset of the catchall term BDSM, age play is defined by the Center for Sexual Pleasure and Health as "sexual role-playing where one partner pretends to be older and in control while the other pretends to be much younger." This could mean fantasizing about being siblings, or teacher and student. According to *The*

Toybag Guide to Age Play by Lee Harrington, the most popular form is parent-child. People like it for all sorts of reasons: the taboo factor; to be silly, to give up control, to explore an inner identity, to enjoy "never having to grow up." I'd heard of it, but it definitely didn't sound like my thing.

It's not that I don't love dirty words and role-play. I can get off on being called a "bad girl," "slut" and "whore" (consensually) by a dominant partner. I've spanked and been spanked by men and women. But this was new to me. Pretending to be someone's mommy? I was on the steep end of that sexual learning curve. How could I do this without sounding idiotic, even if only to my-self? It was like entering an entirely new world, a sci-fi universe being made up on the spot.

Still, there is a critical moment in bed when a partner shares his deepest fantasy, and you can either tell him you're not into it—or you can go with it. I chose the latter.

Why did I say yes? I was flattered that he felt comfortable enough to share that side of his psyche with me. I don't know how often he goes there with lovers, but it's obviously riskier than admitting you're into light bondage. I also liked the idea of having the power to control exactly what would happen between us; I could tell him he was, indeed, being a good boy for me, or that he wasn't, and would need correcting. The roles set clear boundaries: I was in charge, and even though I'm more inclined to be on the receiving end of orders given in bed, I can get off on being in command, perhaps because I know what being on the other side is like.

He'd already told me that his mom had passed away when he was a child, and you don't have to be Freud to figure that one out. My heart went out to him for losing his mom so early in life. I was also relieved that whatever happened between him and me,

I'd never have to meet the woman I was "playing." I couldn't help but feel a tug at my heartstrings for this big "baby."

By submitting to me in this way, he was the opposite of the macho, selfish guys I'd dated who wanted everything their way or never dared show me their most private selves. One of the things I enjoy most about sex is the sense of connection where nothing is held back. If agreeing to be his "mommy" would get me to that place, I was game. I had long been a champion of people baring their deepest fantasies. You can't do that in a half-assed way.

Still, I was pretty sure I wouldn't like it. How wrong I was. As he lay on top of me, he sucked on my nipples in a manner no lover ever has. He wasn't sucking on them to give me pleasure; his tongue never brushed against my nipple to find out if it was hard. He sucked in a fast, loud way, like a baby would to get milk, cheeks moving with exaggerated motions in and out. He wanted attention as much as TLC. It was fascinating, because it felt entirely different than the usual sensual act. Here was a man over six feet tall who probably weighed close to two hundred pounds, yet he seemed to have shrunk as he curled himself up against me (I'm around five-foot-three and one hundred and fifty pounds). He felt smaller as he "nursed." He was showing me his vulnerability, transforming into someone else, which made me want to offer up a different side of myself in return. And that was hot.

But the real surprise—which may be the most disturbing part, or the most honest, depending on your perspective—is what the age play stirred up in me. At thirty-six, I don't have any children, but I want them badly. "Baby fever" hardly begins to describe it. If I could pick up a baby at the supermarket along with my groceries, I would. And this unlikely sexual dynamic, the big baby literally calling me "mommy," called forth powerful caretaking feelings. It was nice, for a short period of time, to be a mother, even a mock one.

Let me be clear: my maternal yearnings in and of themselves are not sexual. But my desire to comfort others does play a role in my sex life. Nurturing has been one of the gifts I pride myself on providing to lovers. That might mean surprising them with dessert, sending them a list of the broken links on their website, giving an intense massage, mailing a package for them, or washing their dishes. Even when I'm in a dominant sexual role, there's an element of caretaking involved. If I'm slapping or spanking or biting or pinching someone who gets off on me delivering pain, I am fulfilling a sexual need. It may not be the same as feeding them chicken soup, but it is still a form of taking care of them.

So while overt mommy play was new to me, combining kink and nurturing wasn't. But this scenario brought my previous experience to a whole new level of intensity. We spun a fantasy in which I was sitting in a hotel bathtub, warm and full of bubbles, while he waited to towel me off, then gave me a foot massage. The stories we shared were far from depraved; they were gentle, tender, loving. I could see myself soaking in that tub, him washing my hair, stroking my feet, fetching food for me, sleeping at the foot of the bed. The sweetness offset the weirdness for me.

But it was a lot to process on a second date, or even a seventieth. This wasn't the kind of sex you enjoy and then forget about. Going to such a deeply psychological head space was overwhelming, especially because we didn't stop to talk about it before or after.

We engaged in role-playing sex two more times over the course of that night and the next morning. I suspected that might be the only way he could get off. I began to wonder how long I could keep this up: I could do it for another date or two, but what would happen after that? What would happen if we really did have kids?

I never had to face that question, however, because after our date, I stopped hearing from him. Save for one brief email check-in, he was gone. I'm too stubborn and proud to beg someone to contact me, so I waited to hear from him. Maybe he felt ashamed about what we'd done, or regretted how much he'd revealed; it was impossible to know. All I knew was the comfort I could take in this: no matter how old I get, sex always has new things to teach me.

Dear John

Lori Selke

Dear John,

 Excuse me. I mean:

 Dear Leather Community,

 No, that's not right either. I mean:

 Dear Leather Scene,

 I don't know quite how to tell you this. I hope it doesn't come as a shock when I suggest that it's high time that we took a good long look at our relationship and acknowledged the truth—we've grown apart, and we continue to head in different directions. Although I am still fond of you and you'll always be an important part of my life, at this stage, it's probably best if, from here on out, we became just friends.

 It wasn't always like this, of course, and I will always treasure the memories I have of us together. Especially those first whirlwind months and years. I really thought it was the kind of match that was meant to last. And it did last—almost two decades. We definitely had some good times together, I won't deny it.

I remember vividly the first time we were introduced. It was in a queer women's support group at college. I was told by the facilitator, a woman only a year or two older than I, that anyone who used any toys or props or costumes during sex could be considered a leatherdyke. Oops! I knew instantly that we belonged together. So glad to make your acquaintance, ma'am.

I met one of the women in that support group again, a few years later, on the end of a very long leash on the Washington DC mall. But I'm getting ahead of myself.

I started writing you love poetry. In fact, I wrote a whole cycle and turned it in as my final project for my queer studies class in college. Somewhere in my boxes of papers I still have those poems, with titles like "The Leatherdyke Meets the Animal Liberationist" and "Boiling Dildos in the Spaghetti Pot" and "Handcuffs" and "Dental Dams in the Midwest." I hope you didn't find them too corny at the time.

I began stalking you, just a little bit. I bought copies of the original, super-kink-friendly lesbian sex magazine *On Our Backs* whenever I could find them in central Michigan. I spent a lot of time sitting next to one slim shelf at the bookstore that for some reason housed Pat (now Patrick) Califia and *The Lesbian S/M Safety Manual*, plus a lot of Victorian spanking porn that I never really looked much at, I'm afraid. Maybe that was a mistake.

But I was young and in love, and I felt so, so alone without you. You were close, but not close enough. I spent hours on the phone with a very sweet couple who lived about two hours away and tried to hook me up with local resources. They answered my questions and recommended books and asked if I had any access to the Internet. This was long before the Web, by the way, before

AOL, just a little after BBS's were all the rage. I did have access to the Internet, thanks to my college email account.

So I started reading and participating in a little group called alt.sex.bondage. And I met so many friends there! They were still all so far away, but at least we were talking to each other at last.

One strange thing about this, though, was that people were always stunned that I went by my real name on these groups. *What's your scene name?* they would ask. *What's your handle?* I'd never even had a childhood nickname, so this was all very confusing to me.

Nonetheless. I moved to Chicago and continued to flirt with you. And you seemed to like me, too. We had a great time once a year at International Mr. Leather, strolling through the vendor area. I met a cute faggy top with a new tongue piercing and a real mean streak in all the right places—he showed me how painful a Wartenberg pinwheel can be when it's used just under the armpit. He didn't want to have sex with me, but brunch he could swing.

The cigar daddy, too—he invited me to his club dinner, sat me down at the big table in the private back room at Ann Sather's Swedish Diner, handed me a stogie and gallantly cut the tip off. He lived in New York, though, so I only saw him once a year or so. He taught me the hand trick. Ask me to show it to you sometime.

And there was that March on Washington I mentioned—where I think we might have gotten to know each other better if it hadn't been for that terrible sunburn—and the year after that, the Stonewall anniversary celebration in New York City.

I think that's when we started seriously dating, yes? When I sat in the fisting workshop held by Carol Queen and Robert Lawrence. When the very tall woman from San Francisco snapped her bullwhip down the aisle of another workshop session. When

I sat next to all those men in their leathers, with their Kaposi's Sarcoma lesions spotting their arms and face. When I ate brunch with a man who called himself Mr. Benson, which sounds like the height of arrogance until you actually met him. If you know what I mean.

During the march proper, we linked arms in a big circle around that tall woman and her bullwhip so that she could march undisturbed by overzealous safety monitors. Remember? I do. I was falling in love. I was crushed out on every single person in that circle. In some ways, I still am.

That was about the same time I went to Boston and met another lovely fag top who saw me standing alone at the bar, introduced himself to me, determined that we had a mutual friend, and then took me into the back room of the Ramrod. Just to watch—he wasn't into girls, after all. We joked about the backroom policy, which was shirtless or leather, and how freaked-out all those lovely butch men would be if I chose the first option. But I was wearing my leather jacket that night, and even though it was quite, quite warm in that back room, I kept it on so that I could spend just a few more minutes watching the men touch each other in ways that I wanted to touch and be touched, too. I was still content to watch. This time.

We had a little long-distance thing going for a while. I would sometimes stop off at the leather bar on the other side of town— the one located in an alley behind a bathhouse. They had a monthly women's night, and I'd risk being stranded or having to pay for a very expensive taxi out of a very tight income just to drink a beer at the bar and chat with other women wearing their bar vests and motorcycle jackets.

Then I moved to San Francisco, and our relationship deepened. It was definitely a love match. I met so many friends and lovers here. I was invited to play parties, I was invited to munches, I met a girl who loved to be spanked and we picked out dildos together and she ate pretzel nuggets out of a bowl on the floor of a kitchen that didn't even belong to me and she wiggled that delicious butt at me while she did it.

I guess this was the honeymoon period. We had a good, long honeymoon, we did. I even had several jobs where I could proudly proclaim myself a "professional pervert." I went from attending play parties to running them. I got some very naughty stories about you and me published. Some of those stories were nominated for awards.

It was at the play parties that I first began to notice some things.

I was booking space for an upcoming party. All I needed to know were the house rules, the rental rates and could we bring some mattresses in to increase the horizontal space? And the owners looked at me kind of funny, and then started talking to me in a way that made me realize that they thought I wasn't really kinky at all, because who combines sex with spanking and bondage? It must mean I wasn't serious about what I was doing and needed some remedial lectures in safer sex, hygiene, and kink, all at once.

This was not cool. We'd known each other for so long. How could you treat me this condescendingly, just because of my orgasms?

Maybe it was a mistake, I rationalized. One bad apple, one unfortunate moment. Everybody makes mistakes.

But then I started noticing some other things. Like the fact that whenever I saw men and women playing together, it seemed the women were on their knees sucking cock a very disproportionate amount of the time. I mean, as in five or six couples surrounding me and my partner, all doing the exact same scene.

And when it wasn't cocksucking, it was young thin women being wound in yards and yards of rope by older bearded men. And when I mentioned all this in bewilderment—remembering the days when most of the tops were women, actually, and most of the bottoms were men, and when had that changed?—people got into shouting matches with me. I was being mean, I was told. I was saying Their Kink Was Not Okay. The cardinal sin.

People started frowning at me when I laughed in the dungeon. Or when I talked dirty to my partners. That was chatting and it wasn't allowed; it was disruptive. My hand could be four fingers up her twat and I'd still be called out for it.

I've also never forgotten the woman in a very expensive custom corset who apparently thought a good way to flirt with me would be to say, "You don't look dressed for the evening," when I showed up at a party in black jeans and T-shirt—perfectly okay by party rules, but apparently not up to her stringent standards.

I don't know what happened. But it had become clear that you and I were growing apart.

I started joking to people about how I wasn't really a pervert, I just liked rough sex. (And knives. And needles. And the smell of leather, and spanking cute girls, and who am I really kidding never mind.) I stopped attending quite as many munches and those play parties. And classes. And clubs.

See, my kinky leather identity grew firmly out of my queerness and my feminism. All three of those elements are important and in some ways inseparable. It's important to me to pursue the sort of social justice that ensures that our consensual relationships are someday entered into from a place of roughly equal societal power. Without that aim, we're simply perpetuating oppression.

Let me be clear: I am not saying that we need to wait until

after the revolution to have the kind of sex and/or play that we want. I'm saying that we cannot turn a blind eye to the institutionalized power imbalances that affect our interpersonal relations when we're negotiating our consensual power exchanges. To do so is venal and corrosive. To do so with a shrug and a nod to the tired catchphrase "your kink is 'kay" is offensive.

There, I said it.

And the last time I said it, you laughed at me. Mocked me publicly, and turned your back on me. When you weren't loudly denouncing me as the PC police, that is.

And I wish I could say I saw it coming, but I didn't. It was a stiletto-heeled kick to my gut.

And after policing my public scenes for years for being too loud, too verbal, filled with too many orgasms and not enough toys, too joyous and not nearly serious enough, where the hell do you get off pretending that I'm the no-fun patrol?

And that's why I'm writing you this letter, leather community. Because if that's really the way you feel about me, then I think it's past time we parted ways. It's not just the one thing, it's an accumulation of tiny estrangements that I can't look past any longer. And it may be my imagination, but it certainly appears that you feel much the same way. We have a long, florid, glorious history together. But I don't think we really like very much who we've both become over the years.

I can't change my history. I can't walk away from it. And I want to be clear that I'm not trying to. I'm not repudiating you or my time with you. I will always be queer and kinky and kinky and queer, and queer kinky perverts will always have a place in my heart and my home—and, let's face it, my bed. (And on my spanking bench, and sitting at my feet...) And I'm always going to find boys and girls wrapped in cowhide pretty fucking hot.

But when it comes to the larger, "pansexual" leather community? Look, it's time we both admit it: the spark is gone.

I need to take care of myself first. And though it pains me to admit it, in this case, that means I need to walk away before we hurt each other further.

I hope you'll always remember me fondly. I'm confident you'll find someone else once we've moved on who's a more compatible match in the long run. It's been fun, hasn't it? We had a good ride, you and I. But it's time to unbuckle the harness, lift the safety bar and step out of the car.

Best wishes and good-bye,
Lori

Sex by Any Other Name
Insiya Ansari

It was two in the morning, and I was frolicking on an air mattress in the middle of my living room with a guarded man. We'd met a month earlier while I was on a work-related trip. After an extended period of phone flirtation, he had flown in from the other end of the state for the weekend so that we could get to know each other better in person.

At the beginning of his trip, we were just friends, but by the third night, we'd advanced to benefits. We were fondling and flattering each other to a soundtrack of hungry, labored respiration, when he bumped up against the sexual glass ceiling that had loomed over all my serious relationships to date.

We'd been chatting between kisses, and the interstitial conversation had just turned to sex. I delivered the bombshell: I'd been with my last boyfriend for five years and we had never done it. The groping froze. A moment later, he proclaimed firmly, "Well, that definitely ain't me." Meaning: *I'd never wait five years for sex with any woman*—capisce? The familiar acidic disappointment hit my gut, and then I felt indignant. A slow-unfolding relationship wouldn't satisfy this one, even if biding his time without sex meant he could end up with a queen like me.

I am a girl with an ample sense of self-worth. I possessed it even during my awkward teenage years, because I was cosseted and adored by my family. Unlike those of many other first-generation American Muslim girls, my parents didn't impose rules to mirror the strictures of their own upbringings in India (which had, nonetheless, been forward-thinking for their time). I hadn't been reduced to sneaking around with boyfriends, and my parents even tolerated it when those boys were "Americans," as they referred to anyone who was either white or black.

With these affordances, I cycled through at least one boyfriend every year. But each relationship played out in my home, under the watchful eyes of my parents, who allowed us to hang there only if my bedroom door was wide open. One of these boyfriends, a chocolate-brown South Indian whom my father dismissed as a raffish thug, managed to get me alone in his bedroom regularly during my sophomore year in high school. He'd ease me onto the bed hopefully, and we'd kiss and grind, never even toying with the button of his baggy purple denim shorts.

About a half hour of that would bring us to the outer limits of my sexual concession zone. I'd unfailingly extract myself with a semiapologetic smile and walk down the hill to my parents' house. This relative chastity was a direct outgrowth of parental enmeshment, as described by a crude maxim in our dialect that essentially means I was "all up in my parents' armpits." Collective values went unspoken. I understood that unlike for the loose Americans I'd grown up around, having sex was tantamount to growing dreadlocks, stretching my earlobe with a gauge or declaring myself agnostic. And I'd never experienced any counterpressure that was convincing enough to make me disrespect my parents. Therefore, I never had to endure that most embarrassing of parent-adolescent rituals, "The [don't get pregnant, use a condom] Talk."

My parents have always called themselves liberal Muslims. While I was growing up, they prayed *namaz* about as often as they drank beer and wine—neither was a regular practice, nor occasioned only by a holiday—and they paid interest on our home. These behaviors countered conventional orthodoxy; some are considered *haram*. My parents weren't the sort to play the "because I said so" card, and for the most part, my brother and I didn't push the limits. But bohemian and secular my parents were not. They were devout believers in the Qur'an's historical narrative, and their cultural values were dictated by an Islamic worldview that was shared throughout our community, a close-knit Shiite minority sect. Within the extended community, news of a hellion child spread fast. I was not very newsworthy until, at eighteen, I met my first love.

Much as I cherished the notion that my relationship with Michel was a love for the ages, it looked a lot like a pop-culture trope: Virginal, Coddled Ingenue Gets Stars Crossed with Dangerous/Broken Casanova. (See: *Grease, Dirty Dancing*, various Molly Ringwald flicks.) I met him in a program that attracted young writers from divergent backgrounds. He'd throw smoldering looks across the room, before he turned his attention to our peers in the program and let rip with impossibly confident, cogent rants about everything from criminal justice to teen moms to the conspicuous consumerism of his broke friends dizzied by their obsession with the latest Jordans. Michel had nearly been denied his high school diploma because of a pitiful attendance record, but I wasn't alone in believing that he was brilliant.

Initially, I was much more taciturn than he was in those meetings, slightly intimidated by the big personalities and strong opinions. When Michel first began flirting with me, I assumed it was because I was fresh meat. When we weren't at work on projects, the testosterone-amped office atmosphere regressed to locker-room antics, the boys assiduously ranking each girl's dateability.

But when Michel and I were together, he'd lose the machismo. He'd make himself vulnerable, dropping his lids over huge, almond-shaped eyes to fully appreciate an affecting song on the radio, while urging me to do the same. He was genuinely present, and I responded with rapt attention. We were both as inquisitive as we were voluble, and a conversation that started with the typical exchange of childhood anecdotes would spiral out into a full-throated debate that folded in topics from gangsterism to interracial dating to international water rights to maternal attachment. He told me that I was the first girl with whom he wanted to talk as often as he wanted to kiss. And I was a "faith over fuck-ups" type, constantly expressing my confidence that he could climb out of hood life to attain the professional victories that he dreamed of.

My parents, in our first truly painful schism, decided Michel was a scoundrel the first time they met him. As I became more wayward, serially ditching my college classes, they blamed him for sucking me into his vortex of troublemaking. They didn't appreciate his intelligence. Rather, my father seemed to feel Michel was too slick—even when, or maybe because—he stooped his long neck, softened his voice, and answered questions with "Yes, sir… no, sir."

I, on the other hand, was outright disrespectful, challenging my parents to "Give me just one reason!" why they didn't like him, and becoming sullen when they came up with five or more. I began to stay out until dawn, sometimes leaving the house just a few hours later with no more than ten words to my parents in between.

Even as Michel's appearance in my life felt transformative, my parents' concerns about our differences weren't entirely off the mark. We were each bewildered by the other's sexual values. Michel was a monument to virility, a player's playa. I made it clear at the beginning of our relationship that I was "waiting until I was married" to have sex. Never mind that the notion of marriage was an abstraction to me. All I knew with certainty was that it was a handy demarcation for the Before and After of sexual intimacy. My sexual values had never caused problems in my relationships before, and since I didn't know what we were missing, I never knew how much I was asking Michel to give up.

This presented a moral quandary for Michel, since he was falling in love with me, despite my abstinence. To attest to how smitten he was, he'd describe his peers' reactions when they heard that Michel was in a celibate relationship: "You, patna? C'mon." "So, y'all still ain't fucked?" They were counting down to the day when I'd inevitably give in to Michel's charms. He was magnetic and sexually experienced in equal measure. He'd begun having sex when he was fifteen. Before he knew of my jealous streak, which was voracious for anecdotes of past girlfriends to obsess over, he'd share tantalizing details, curious to see my reaction. He told me a story about being jailed briefly, and then released in the middle of the night. Hungry for sex, he sought relief with a repulsive-looking girl from the neighborhood known for her loose standard. Although the anecdote shocked me, it also comforted me as I placed it squarely in the rearview: I figured that was the kind of behavior that he had gotten out of his system after all his teenage exploits. Unfortunately, it wasn't.

It took only six months for Michel to begin cheating—at least, as far as I was able to trace. But it took a year before I was faced with evidence that, even through my fog of infatuation, was undeniable. I caught a friend of his in a lie about a night they'd supposedly been together, when I called to inquire about the friend's injury. Short of his saying, "What broken leg?" everything about his response made it clear the story was a cover-up.

The truth tumbled out over the phone while Michel was out of town. He was in the rural South, helping a friend relocate from California. I was still at college and living at home with my parents. Unwilling to wait for him to return, I made my first big purchase on a credit card to fly out to meet him and seek an answer for my bewilderment. I held on to a faint hope that the irregular phone connection had produced some grotesque misunderstanding on my part, even though at some point he'd quietly said of the first indiscretion, "Baby, this is just a rock from the mountain of lies that our relationship is built on."

After I arrived, we spent the first night crying, with his head buried in my lap as he apologized again and again. The next day, his friend's batty auntie who lived next door to the guesthouse where he was staying told the rest of her family that we'd spent the night moaning bawdily. In a twisted attempt at defending my honor, Michel poured sugar in her van's gas tank. The engine easily revved to life the next morning and she drove away, leaving us on the lot alone. I spent the morning feeling angry and ashamed. Couldn't she tell the difference between sex and elegiac despair?

Stockholm syndrome is the only plausible psychoanalysis I can come up with for what happened that night, and for my overall reaction to the greatest betrayal I'd experienced. Michel and I were bored and frustrated, stuck in the backcountry without transportation. We'd been staring each other down from opposite ends of the thin mattress, and his explanations for the transgressions hadn't gotten any more coherent—how could they, when the acts were so muddled within his own psyche? I'd pressed him all I could.

Seized with a panicked thought that I would have to return to the generally unchallenging life I'd had without him, I folded myself into his arms. The role reversal commenced in earnest, and suddenly I was the one stroking his brow and kissing him. The warmth turned to heat, and the mutual comforting transitioned into desire. Later that night, we had sex.

Sex. It's been more than ten years since that night, and this unequivocal label still makes me recoil. In my mind, what Michel and I did that night was something different—what a friend later called, "The Dip." I finally let him enter me, but I didn't give in to the throes of unbridled intercourse. It was an approximation: controlled and tentative, and haunted by post-cheating sadness. When I reflected on the "why" soon after, I told myself that some act resembling the sexual activity he was used to would satisfy the desire that had brought us to this point in the first place.

Of course, it was a fool's bargain, a circumscribed compromise that I also assumed would keep me, within the most narrow definitions, a virgin. By then I'd read several novels in which a night like this ended with a white sheet on a backyard clothesline, fluttering in the breeze and dotted with blood: the victory flag of a man newly married to a God-fearing Muslim girl. I threw out the superficial physiology lessons we'd all snickered at in junior-high sex ed and instead called upon this definition, which I took to mean that if there was no penetration, we were still engaging in heavy foreplay and nothing more. So on this night, and a few others, I crossed a line without crossing The Line. We'd be fooling around, and when I thought we were in a danger zone, I'd press my palms to his stomach and guide his body away from me slightly, like intuitive adjustments made to a ship's course according to shifting winds. Most of the people whom I've shared this tale with can't quite believe that I could have been so reckless, and confused, and naive.

Oh, trust me, I tell them. Before that fateful phone call from the South, I had ignored plenty of evidence about Michel's flirtation with other women, because I believed (and still do) that he loved me deeply.

For more than a year, I had watched Michel struggle with his duality: the tender, impassioned humanist, contrasted with the *napuck*, or brat, that my parents had recognized in him from the start. It was contagious; I turned into the poster child for Trying to Please Everyone While Pleasing No One. I was even worse at the balancing act than Michel.

When I was home, I was acutely aware of how disappointed my parents were that I was still dating him, and how they seemed to glower even more when I became antsy to leave, hogging the cordless phone as I checked for messages from you-know-who. When he did call, I'd up and leave at a moment's notice to meet him. I couldn't remember the last time my parents, my brother and I had eaten dinner together as a family.

And what's more, The Dip itself was a bust. There was no freedom in it, and guilt flared up in both Michel and me and repelled us from the temporary bonded state we'd reached. He knew I was unhappy defying my parents, and with him, my suspicion fueled increasingly controlling behavior. Within six months, Michel was cheating again, and more flagrantly than before.

Partly, I stayed so long because I believed my youthful indiscretion would be justified if we managed to stay together and vanquish our obvious incompatibility. After Michel and I had to let go, through my next relationship I tried to vanquish the sex itself.

My next long-term boyfriend was utterly devoted, loving and willing to be patient with me, even in the shell-shocked state I was in after Michel. Our sex life unfolded completely on my terms. I remember reading an article at the time about "born-again virgins"—Christian girls who had sex and then decided to return to abstinence, presumably to reclaim a moral and spiritual high ground. I hated the term but decided to try out the approach.

Like Michel, my new man wasn't Muslim, nor was he otherwise religious, but he was willing to entertain this "born-again" status. He was significantly older and had already been in several long-term relationships. He seemed settled, and he was focused on the horizon, hoping we'd get married. We were together five years, and he was just as devoted to my newfound piety as I was, never once implying that I'd lose him if I didn't loosen up. But the sexual repression I was imposing on myself didn't feel right. I wish I could say that from being with Michel, I'd gained clarity that sex before marriage is ruinous. But it taught me more about what I *didn't* believe: that because I had pushed up against a prohibition, I'd also traded in my status as an observant Muslim.

That's not because I took issue with Islamic precepts around premarital sex, like some of my friends, who wrote them off as irrelevant to their modern lives. I just wasn't convinced that this one transgression negated all my other religious virtues.

In that sense, getting right with God was the easy part. But the post-Michel celibacy wasn't driven by conviction—it was a shelter under which I could heal, without having to reconcile my past experimentation with a religious and sexual practice that would feel right moving forward.

Ten years after Michel, I came to the brink again, faced with the toll of the hard work I'd shirked. This time, it was with the guy on the air mattress. A year after we met, the struggle over sex was again driving a wedge in our relationship. He was asking for an open relationship, and rather than feel the pain of that betrayal, I decided to go whole hog. I gave him everything that I'd physically withheld in my prior relationships.

At first, my heart wasn't in the decision, and the fact that I wasn't holding anything back scared me a bit. This anxiety begat paranoia. How could the man really love me and at the same time pressure me to have sex when I felt so ambivalent about it? Was this my pattern: becoming infatuated with selfish men who would do me wrong? I dizzied myself with these thoughts, and gave of myself tentatively. Moreover, the sex was often disappointing.

So it might sound delusional when I say that I considered our intimacy over the next five years to be redemptive. But finally confronting the ambiguity in my sex life allowed me to be more accepting of all my purported contradictions. And when the obsession with my sexual status fell away, my religious identity came into relief. I focused on maintaining the practices that are core to my spirituality and my connection to God.

Ultimately, when Air Mattress Man and I fell apart, I didn't regret what I'd chosen. So much for that compartmentalized existence that parents, and many men, would like to impose: the idea that a good Muslim girl doesn't engage in sex before she's committed for life. It's a specter I'm glad to be rid of. Here, finally, was that unambiguous status I'd been refusing to claim. I'm an unmarried, Muslim nonvirgin. I've said it aloud; still, I don't disappear.

Enhancing Masochism:
How to Expand Limits and Increase Desire
Patrick Califia

It was the third SM play party I had ever attended. Since I was one of the organizers, it was up to me (and my cohost) to get things started, even though I was barely more experienced at group sex than most of the guests. That lovely lady (let's call her Fanny) was gracious enough to let me drag her into the center of the room and tie her up on all fours. She was a slender redhead with Celtic knots tattooed on her shoulders. The brightly entwined lines morphed into plants and fantastical animals as the design spilled onto her upper arms. She had long, very curly red hair, so she looked like a Raphaelesque angel you had divested of its robe and got ass-up and begging for cock. Like magic, as soon as we took off some of our clothes, everybody else formed couples and triads and got out their toys.

Fanny really, really, really wanted me to put my biggest strap-on in her ass. I did preliminary play with my fingers, an ass plug, and my second-biggest dildo. I massaged her, talked dirty to her, slipped lube into her butt, and played with her nipples. But her ass would only open so far. We had reached a plateau.

My pervy little angel was whispering something. Given the volume of the music and other players, the only thing I could hear was "Please, Sir." I leaned forward, but I couldn't get close enough to her head to decipher the whole message while I was manipulating a slender vibrator in her butt.

"Speak up!" I finally roared, letting a little of my frustration show in my voice.

"Get my belt!" she shouted, matching my volume. Apparently she was feeling a bit more frustrated than I was.

A passerby was kind enough to find her jeans and tug her simple leather belt out of the loops. I put down the vibes and plugs and dildos and picked up the supple length of that ordinary article of clothing. Suddenly it seemed vested with power and fear, an implement that might help us cross the line into a new realm of experience. I doubled it up and smacked her with it, drawing a broad red stripe across her pale, shapely ass, increasing the force until she was shuddering and dragging on the ropes. She had told me that she liked pain, but I didn't really get it until I saw her clawing at the leather tabletop, having what looked and sounded like an orgasm.

After that, we had no trouble getting my fat, ten-inch cock into her ass. She was as relaxed as could be. And if she did begin to tense up, all I had to do was trail the belt down her buttocks, pressing gently on her welts, to make her sigh and melt into me. It was a grand fuck, one of my first experiences with combining pain and pleasure, doing a scene that looked vanilla but most certainly was not.

Would this technique work with anybody? No. You have to

start with at least some of the hardwiring for masochism. If you do have that hardwiring, should you be expected to stand up and get bullwhipped for an hour, with no warm-up, to entertain a crowd at a leather community fund-raiser for breast cancer? Only if you are an exceptionally heavy player and such an exhibitionist that nothing matters but the spectators. But can you perhaps learn to take a bit more, and then a bit more, to please a lover and yourself? Yes.

Some Definitions

In this article I use the term *masochism* to refer to the desire and the ability to become aroused and perhaps even climax while experiencing sensations that other people avoid. Although I talk about pain and discomfort, it should be understood that once a masochist is aroused and in a state of surrender to these intense sensations, they are not experiencing the kind of pain that someone who is ill or traumatized feels when they are shocked by how torturous it can be to have a body. I also want to note that there are masochists who seek out pain even if it does not arouse them; willingly tolerating hurt can have a number of positive results, which will be clear a little further on.

Unfortunately, the stigma of the label *masochism* has been perpetuated by sex-negative doctors, psychologists and other mental health "professionals" whose vocabularies lack precision. So-called experts get away with claiming that masochism is unhealthy because they use the term loosely to describe other types of human behavior as well. Patients who stay in violent relationships, allow themselves to be exploited by employers or family members, can't take control over their own lives, or harm themselves physically and emotionally are referred to as exhibiting masochism. Most of these people haven't got a kinky bone in their bodies. Yet people who enjoy being spanked, whipped, pinched, bitten, et cetera because it gives them an erotic rush and makes them feel closer to their partners are also called masochists.

This flawed logic has resulted in the diagnosis "sexual masochism" appearing in the *Diagnostic and Statistical Manual-IV TR (DSM-IV-TR)*, the industry standard for mental-health bureaucracy. "Sexual sadism" is in there, too. You can't write a case report, create a treatment plan, or (most importantly) bill an insurance company without using the *DSM's* nomenclature of supposed dysfunction.

Is there any objective proof that people who get wet during a spanking are also getting ripped off financially, intimidated by bullies, anorexic, being battered, or likely to engage in self-mutilation? No. And there never will be, because we are conflating two separate categories of human experience. One is a sexual identity or experience; the other is a state of disenfranchisement, oppression, traumatization, or self-hatred. People consent to the former; they wish they could escape the latter. The earliest attempts to educate mental-health professionals about BDSM focused on the fact that this was a sexual style based on consent and negotiation. These were pleasurable acts committed by adults who chose to enjoy kinky sex. This message reached a certain number of people. But it is very difficult to overturn generations of fear and disgust. For many "experts" whose credentials allowed them to pronounce on our mental health (or sickness), the fact that people would consent to do these things became proof that BDSM players had to be mentally ill. If you weren't crazy, this reasoning goes, you wouldn't want to do these things or agree to have them done to you. For therapists who are judgmental about sexual variation, the fact that someone would consent to wearing a pair of nipple clamps or having their face slapped just proves that they are indeed sick and unable to distinguish between healthy and unhealthy experiences. And the person who does such awful things to them is a monster.

For alleged social scientists to judge human sexuality this way is embarrassing. The assumption that variant sexualities are mental illnesses has more to do with conservative religious values than it does with objective observation. If a mental state or human behavior is unhealthy, we ought to be able to demonstrate that it makes that person unhappy, interferes with their ability to give and receive love, prevents them from setting goals that give them a sense of fulfillment, and injures their health. It's not enough to say BDSM is sick or crazy because most people don't do it. Most people don't become concert pianists or Olympic athletes, either. These are individual dreams of excellence that cause people to devote a great deal of time and effort to perfecting their abilities. If you took away the opportunity to compete in their chosen field, these "minority members" would be devastated. Does that prove they are addicted or coerced into loving classical music or diving from high places? You can see how this line of thinking breaks down if we ask some reasonable questions.

This is not to say that BDSMers (or our relationships) are always happy and strong. Our community has its share of people who are mean-spirited or manipulative or crackers. Some of us find romantic love and lots of sex with ease; others experience higher levels of loneliness and unsatisfied desire. But this is simply the human condition. It's okay for us to be imperfect. We struggle, like anyone else, to figure out what sort of relationships are ethical or will meet our needs, how to communicate unwelcome information to a partner, whether to let a conflict result in separation or rededication to the relationship. That doesn't prove that we are sick or crazy. As long as we are conscious of our own and others' well-being, and striving to contribute to that, we are on a good path and we don't need to engage in harmful self-criticism.

An Alternative View of Masochism

How many times have you heard someone say, "Pain is a warning that our bodies are in danger"? It sounds like a truism. But, like most assumptions, it deserves a closer look. While pain can be a symptom of disease or injury, human beings have always sought to control their reaction to pain. If we couldn't tolerate at least some discomfort, sadness, anxiety, or less-than-wonderful physical states, how would any of us get through an ordinary day—much less deal with hard work or a chronic illness?

For millions of years, people have deliberately constructed painful situations and faced them to obtain a number of different benefits. In some societies, painful ordeals or body modification mark an individual's transition from childhood to adulthood. Obtaining spiritual guidance has often required a sacrifice, to prove the seriousness of one's intent and create an altered state that allows communication between this world and other realms. Consciously choosing to suffer discomfort has resulted in the acquisition of wisdom, experiencing divine rapture, obtaining healing, and locating and killing meat for the cooking pot. Whether the goal is mundane or transcendental, the ability to use our hearts and minds to convince our bodies to continue to function while we are aching (or worse) is the hallmark of courage, loyalty and strength.

One of the most painful physical events a human being can endure is the birth of a child. Are women "masochistic" because they endure pregnancy and birth?

The rituals and other trials I described above are not examples of sexual masochism. But they highlight the physiological reasons why it's possible for us to get aroused by pain. When our bodies feel stress, they autonomously produce chemicals that help us cope. We may pant, bringing extra oxygen into our bodies. Adrenaline, endorphins and natural narcotics flood our nervous system. Euphoria and agony are next-door neighbors—you can't break that paradoxical connection. And if you are not willing to tolerate contradictions and paradoxes, human behavior will never make much sense to you.

Postindustrial Western societies romanticize sex. To some extent, this is good. I wouldn't want to go back to a time when premarital sex hardly existed, women had no sexual autonomy and marriages were arranged by the couple's families. Falling in love is a good reason to be together, even if its initial intensity can rarely be sustained forever.

We've come to expect a level of intimacy and understanding or rapport, especially in the first stages of sexual experience, that very few lovers can sustain. Some women's first experience of intercourse is easy; others feel varying degrees of twinginess or even a stab of pain when the hymen is broken. But even after that inconvenience is eliminated, it takes some practice for two bodies (especially two bodies of dissimilar gender) to create a mutual rhythm of lovemaking. Being able to tolerate discomfort or even get turned on by it may be one of the things that helps us put up with each other long enough to get better at providing pleasure.

On an online message board for kinky women, a conversation took place about why experiencing pain makes some women get wet. In less civilized times, getting hurt might be a signal that sexual assault was going to occur. One or two of them speculated that this reflex might have helped their gender survive rape.

I have no idea whether most women or only a handful get physically excited by roughness or pain. Even if this reaction occurs, it does not justify violence against women. Rape is evil because it involves using another's body as if they were an object, ignoring the person inside and their response to it. Most of the time, rape is an unpleasant and squalid experience that has no pleasurable content. But even if rape results in an orgasm for the victim, I assert that it is as evil to give someone an orgasm against their will as it is to fuck them while preventing them from coming.

We like to think of pleasure as good and pain as bad, but the Shadow side of us sees through that simplistic thinking. I have seen more hatred expressed in an act of vanilla sex than I could believe, and I have seen inexpressible tenderness while one partner bled and the other inhaled their pain like the bouquet of a rare wine.

Who's There?
This "big picture" stuff is fun to think about, discuss and research. But it's a little too abstract to help two people who want to branch out in the bedroom and get into some daunting activities. How can you make your socially unacceptable, thigh-squeezing, nubby-nippled, ball-tightening dreams come true?

It helps to give some preliminary thought to the psychology of both top and bottom. When I do workshops on BDSM role-playing, I like to give participants four different scales that they can use to rate themselves, for masochism, sadism, submission and dominance. Each of these qualities is independent of the others. I've met dominant masochists and submissive sadists, for example.

Why someone is going to inflict or accept a sensation is as important as who will be playing each part. A masochist may be willing to pretend they are submissive just so they can get whipped till they cry. Without the catharsis of a good workout on a regular basis, the masochist gets cranky and sluggish and depressed. As long as they are black-and-blue, they are perky and industrious. You may get more out of a masochist if you dispense with courtesies such as waiting at the table or picking up heavy things and letting them tell you which implements they adore, which ones they laugh at and which ones strike terror into their hearts. I've seen joyous and amazing pain play that had not a shred of role-playing in it. (This does not mean, by the way, that a masochist cannot be quite loyal and helpful to you, if only because you see and value a side of them that the world despises.)

A submissive may not like pain at all unless it is presented as a service that they are required to perform for the master or mistress. It is the submissive's obligation to provide service and give pleasure—to yield and submit to a higher will. Pain can be administered as a symbol of ownership. "I can do this to you because you belong to me, and you will take it because it excites and relaxes me."

If you don't know where you fit in this complex picture, don't worry about it too much. It can take a lot of experience to figure out your own psychic twists and turns. Very few of us are exclusively top or bottom. If there wasn't at least a crumb of masochism in the sadist, how could he or she understand what they are asking the bottom to do? Not to mention the fact that people's needs often change as life changes them.

Even if you know your pain tolerance can be rated on the heavy end of the scale, be prepared for its fickleness. There will be nights when the paddle that you worshipped last time is just too evil to be borne. Remember that the point of doing a scene is how it makes you feel, not the techniques or toys being used. A good top understands this, and won't throw a hissy if you need to be beaten with a terry-cloth bathrobe tie.

I hope it won't completely confuse the issue to say that not all pain trips require a top and a bottom. Some people who create ordeals view themselves as spiritual guides or assistants; they don't want a romantic relationship. I've heard hot stories of two competitive bottoms who got together to see who would use their safeword first. And, during those periods of drought when the bars and parties and clubs seem populated by toads and trolls, the self-infliction of sexy pain is a very nice adjunct to masturbation. Who could you trust more than yourself?

Set and Setting

The terms *set* and *setting* were coined by Timothy Leary to describe factors that determine the experience of ingesting psychedelic drugs. It is useful to consider these factors because they influence the emotional content of an event, whether it is theater, long-distance running or therapy. Set has to do with the participants' mind-set, the internal processes that can either enhance or destroy pleasure. Setting refers to the location where the event takes place—what you see, smell, touch, hear and feel around you.

These factors are highly individual. If the steps I suggest don't sound effective for you, you are the best judge of that. But at least I can give you some specific ideas that have proven their worth for me and other players. This can help you pin down your own experimental parameters. And after every session, it's a good idea to discuss what did and didn't work, with an eye to brainstorming new possibilities for erotic play. If you must give your partner negative feedback, express it with tenderness, and surround your misgivings with praise for what did work. Both top and bottom make themselves equally vulnerable in a session. If the only thing you can come up with is a barrage of criticism or inflated demands, the two of you are probably incompatible.

Take a look at the space where the scene is going to happen. Do enough preparation so that the two of you can be spontaneous. Everything you are going to need should be in the room. Leave the room if you must, but be aware you are opening the oven and letting some of the heat out. When you return, you'll need to back up a little and build up to the point you reached when the two of you broke connection.

The room needs to be clean—well, for most fetishes. Toys ought to be organized, in good repair and accessible. Lube and safe-sex barriers should be in clear view. Rope ought to be untangled, clean, inspected for weaknesses and laid out so it won't turn into a snarl the minute the top touches it. If you are going to play with locking devices, make sure there are extra keys, and that both of you know where they are.

Think of this as foreplay. You can start getting excited by your own sexiness, and by anticipating your partner's presence. Touching your toys and disinfecting a play surface is like caressing your own body. Your energy, sense of purpose, or consciousness starts gathering into a focus on Eros.

Before you play, ask yourself what makes you feel alluring and powerful. (I am including bottoms here because you need your own strength. The session comes from you as much as, if not more than, from the top.) Take the time and trouble to dress up, even if you are only wearing a beautiful collar or a badass pair of boots. Get enough rest and eat a healthy meal a couple of hours before you play.

I'm going to assume that you've already been educated about how to negotiate a scene, get any needed consent, choose a safe-word, et cetera. I'm also going to assume that you know your way around the toys or equipment you will use. This is an article about pain play in general; describing every single technique is beyond my scope. Never pretend to have experience that you lack. There is honor only in being honest about this and making sure you get trained to an expert level.

Unless you are the Ice Queen escorting your latest paramour to your frigid palace, I recommend taking the bottom into a warm room. Loose, relaxed muscles are going to accept building sensations more easily. I also suggest taking away one of your bottom's senses, if only for a little while. Using a blindfold or gag is your first demand for control over their body. Can they let go and graciously accede to allowing you to orchestrate their experience?

Take the time to verbally or visually remind the two of you (or your birthday party guests) who it is you are manifesting in this fantasy. In what time or place are you encountering each other? You can do a simple breathing exercise to get grounded in the present. Or perhaps you've constructed an elaborate story with chapters and verses. This provides a meaningful context for pain.

During some sessions, the reason for the infliction of pain is elicited from the bottom while they are under duress ("You're hurting me because I'm a dirty pig!" or "You are giving me pain to push me out of my body, so I can fly free.") In the past, I have said that it is the top's responsibility to determine what each action means and share that significance with the bottom. But I have come to see that finding this underlying meaning is really a joint project. It may be a conspiracy that can be verified by silently meeting each other's eyes, or it may be a sudden revelation that has to be shouted or whispered aloud. You may find the answer in your own heart or see it emerging in the shape of your partner's face. It can be an old friend, an enemy or a complete surprise.

Arousing the bottom is an important first step, unless you are playing with a rare and wonderful creature who needs pain to get aroused. Give your partner a brief massage. Highlight the genitals but don't give them too much attention. You want to create anticipation by teasing. If the bottom has a favorite toy that already gets them going, why not begin with that? Proceed from the familiar to the unfamiliar. Bondage can be very helpful. It allows the bottom to feel contained and secure, and gives them something to pull on when things get exciting.

I dearly love to mix sexual stimulation with gradually increasing levels of pain. I also want to keep the bottom awake and responsive, so I won't use the same implement for too long. If I am whipping someone, I switch between implements that go "thud" and skinny, flexible tools that sting. As blood rises to the surface of the skin, it becomes more sensitive; sometimes running your fingertips or a piece of fur over the skin is exquisite, almost too much so. I also like to vary dry skin versus wet during a whipping or spanking. Generally, wet skin is more sensitive.

Alternating with the bad behavior, I am kissing the bottom, stroking their body, locating various erogenous zones, and titillating them. I want them to need my touch. Winning pleasure is a reward for enduring or enjoying a low level of pain. Be patient with this type of training. It can take several sessions before you begin to see the bottom opening up and allowing you to do more and more. Trust can't always be built in one session.

A bottom who needs safety before they can take down their walls will appreciate being asked how they are doing and reminded that this is all within their control. (It is a common joke among tops who enjoy electrical play that if you give the bottom a control box, they will smartly turn up the dial to levels that were not allowed when the control rested in the top's hand.) You might think that safety is a universal requirement for all masochists, but I have found instead that a certain amount of realism may be necessary to unlock an erotic response to higher levels of pain.

If you really are a captive, you know you will have to take more than the person who is playing at being a captive.

Fear is the most powerful obstacle to building up a tolerance for and erotic response to pain. It may sound corny, but I love to recite the Bene Gesserit rite about pain from the *Dune* novels. Get the bottom to pay attention to what is really going on, right now, rather than their exaggerated and panicky image of what might happen to them. I find that if I can get a bottom to stick with me for the first twenty minutes or so, a whip or a fistful of clothespins suddenly gets a whole lot easier to take. That's because naturally occurring chemicals are beginning to hit the bloodstream, turning "pain" into "wheeee!"

If you are able to feel energy around yourself and your partner, remind them that you want to link the two of you together. I have found that it often works to create a vocal circuit between me and my partner. When I hurt them, they can open their mouth and by panting or making a noise pass the pain on to me. I take the pain, turn it into pleasure, and push it back into them. (I may be pushing other things into them as well, dirty lowlife that I am.) It's amazing how often people will experience exactly what you tell them to feel. If you have a certain destination in mind, take the bottom there, one blow or pinch or slap at a time.

If you are playing with a submissive rather than a pure masochist, you can use service-oriented psychology to build tolerance for pain. As I said earlier, the submissive wants to be possessed and yield to another person; they want to be of service. They will take pain if you make it their job to take it. The pain becomes one item on a menu of conduct or sacrifices that you, the master or mistress, demand because it pleases you. Pain becomes a way to demonstrate your control over him or her. But this may not occur to your submissive unless you spell it out. People tend to get confused during play—they are in an altered state. So speak slowly and use simple words if you feel you are not getting through.

Consensual Nonconsent

For some bottoms, the object of painful techniques is to be out of control. They do not want a cooperative, mutually negotiated scenario, but rather a nonconsensual fantasy and a fair amount of force. Restraints will have to be strong and escape-proof. They need to struggle and suffer until they reach a phase of liberation or release. They may want to be "broken." I urge newer players especially to proceed carefully. The emotional consequences of a session can last long after the toys have been put away. So be cautious of a scene this heavy—do you want to take care of a bottom who has lost their will to you? And if you are a bottom seeking a scene of this nature, please take responsibility for your own feelings and needs. It is unethical to expect a top to take on a larger role in your life than they wish to take. Do not engage in harassment or stalking! If you know you will be vulnerable after a heavy scene, arrange care for yourself before you play, so you don't crash when you are all alone and have no resources to keep you connected to the human race. As sweet as those endorphins are, losing them is a wicked crash.

Many of us associate pain with punishment, and fantasy punishment scenarios abound in BDSM play. There are lots of teachers who paddle unruly students, daddies who have to put little girls (age thirty-two) in the corner, guards who flog convicts who tried to escape, et cetera. Punishment can put the top and bottom in an adversarial dynamic. If this disturbs you, you may want to require the bottom to admit that they deserve the punishment, and aim the scene toward getting them to feel more attached to you. By beating them, you are driving them toward the safe cage of your possessiveness. Or you may find, as a top, that when you are in a certain wicked mood, you don't want to make nice, you just want to kick the shit out of somebody who knows they belong on the floor.

In most scenes that include significant levels of discomfort, the bottom will reach a plateau. There are a number of ways to deal with a bottom who says they can't take any more. One possibility is to take them at their word and praise them for what they were able to do. If you feel that they are capable of more and may be disappointed later if they give up, you may want to simply take a break and see if some comfort and protein can screw up their courage once more. If the bottom told you there were certain things they wanted to experience, and the two of you haven't made that happen yet, they may be motivated to dig a little deeper if you remind them of what their masochistic ambitions were prior to play.

Sometimes people cannot willingly go where they need to go—they have to be taken there. This is a controversial observation, and most people will want to steer clear of it. For most of us, it is safest to stick with the zone of play where we have clear, uncomplicated consent. It's a dicey proposition for a top to ignore a bottom's pleas and continue to hurt them until they yield. You wind up manifesting a great deal of the Shadow, and you'll feel quite a backlash from that.

Once upon a time, play without limits or safewords was very common in the gay men's leather community. A bottom was expected to do some research on a master before approaching him. Did you really want it, or not? If you made a bid for his attention and he took you home, you were supposed to make yourself available for whatever he liked to do. He was God, and you were dirt. Whining later was seen as sissy bullshit. If you whined, no top would touch you—you were an unreliable coward who might make secret and sacred things public to the authorities.

I appreciate the modern, pansexual kinky community's desire to keep BDSM safe, sane and consensual (as the old slogan goes). But I sometimes think we have allowed the pendulum to swing too far in the direction of predictable scenes in which the top functions as an extra pair of hands for the bottom. While it can be a great deal of fun to help your bottom masturbate to their favorite things, is there not some way to make equal space for what the top wants? It is a double bind, being expected to exercise a dark and wonderful power while obsessing with the intricacies of the bottom's sensitivities, perpetually second-guessing them. A lot of the bottoms I meet nowadays seem terribly spoiled to me, and very unhappy, because they don't really want to be running things. More than a few good bottoms in our little world seem lost under the current mores. They long for the thrill of encountering the harsh will of an Other who is severe and powerful. Here's a story about this impasse.

I once participated in a whipping booth at a fund-raiser for the Operation Spanner defendants. (We were raising money for a small, private club of British leathermen who had been arrested and charged with assault for doing consensual SM with each other.) Prospective bottoms were allowed to pick any of several implements and specify the number of strokes and the level of intensity they desired. I was surprised how many eager novices lined up to see what it was all about. This seemed to be a safe way to try new toys and be just a bit of a masochist.

Toward the end of the event, after almost everyone had left, I was ready to pack it in. But one woman was very persistent. When I told her she would not be able to use the tickets she had purchased and offered her a refund, she was quite upset. She told me she had never been caned, she was terrified of it, but she felt so compelled to be caned that she was going out of her mind. She literally begged me to show her what it would be like to be out of control from pain.

So I bent her over the leather whipping bench, held her down with one hand on her lower back, and caned the bejesus out of her. She had asked for a dozen strokes and began to protest when we reached eight. "I have to insist on giving you what you asked for when you first talked to me," I told her, "because I think that is what you really want and need." So I hit her quite hard for the last four strokes, then added an additional one—"So you know that everything is not up to you. Sometimes the top will decide what you get."

She was dizzy when she straightened up, and beaming. So proud of herself and grateful. She fell on my neck and hugged and kissed me. I even got a thank-you card from her years later. Sadly, in all that time, she had encountered no one who would help her over the hump by ignoring her pleas for mercy. What a waste of talent and thrills! Now, there was a potential masochist worth her salt.

But you can see how easily this scenario could have gone all pear-shaped, as our British colleagues would say. If I had been wrong in my assessment of her, she could very easily have come up from the table fighting mad, and justifiably so. She could have accused me of assaulting her. It certainly would have harmed my reputation (such as it is, poor sooty thing) and upset everyone who heard about it. We talk very little, regrettably, about how much the top needs to be able to trust the bottom. Buyer's re-morse can ruin another player's life.

If it makes your crotch tingle to squeeze someone's balls until he protests, or take a sharp little blade to her inner thigh, or if you can't wait to get a blow job after you see the first bruises appear on a healthy pair of buns—well, you are by definition a sadist. The psychiatric experts pity masochists as self-harming fools. But they think sadists are dangerous. The *DSM-IV-TR* has some very silly things to say about sadists becoming rapists and killers.

The vulnerability of the masochist is plain. There they are, perhaps bound, heart pounding, dreading what is going to happen next, promising themselves that if they can just get through this one session they will never ask to be whipped/branded/clipped/pierced/squeezed/frozen/tattooed again. But what about the leather-clad bastard who is going to put this poor, naked person through hell? Never mind that the masochist begged and pleaded for it yesterday. The expense of the equipment, the time it took to locate a soundproof space and good bondage equipment, all this effort is seen as self-serving rather than an honest attempt to make the bottom's dreams come true.

No-Fault Play

It's so easy to make a mistake once play begins. People shut down and quit communicating. In semidarkness, a whip may land where it shouldn't. A game that was great fun two weeks ago is causing flashbacks tonight. The suspension equipment breaks, resulting in a painful fall, or a cane cracks in half and cuts someone. And yet everyone involved in these scenes had the best of intentions, and did everything within reason to be a good play partner.

This is why I recommend a no-fault attitude for BDSM players. As long as both partners respect each other, make a good-faith effort to abide by each other's limits and are open to feedback, I think that missteps ought to be understood as part of the price you pay for being on the edge. Indifferent or bad experiences are there to teach us how to avoid them. A couple or group who have an accident ought to give and receive comfort, make up and keep learning. It takes a lot of experience, and a certain amount of innate talent, to correctly assess and challenge the central nervous system. Luck is a factor as well!

If you take any of the above paragraphs as an excuse for being lazy, negligent, or callous, well, you just ought to go to hell, that's all I have to say. And I'll probably be there to shovel some coal on the blaze.

Enough, Already!

In closing, let me bring up one more controversial fact. The heavier the scene, the more both partners experience weariness, anxiety, and aches and pains. It takes a lot of strength, grace and stamina to work on someone's body for a prolonged period of time. If you are a switch or a top, what is your attitude toward your own pain tolerance? Do you disapprove of it or ignore it? Do you pretend it doesn't exist? Or do you work with it to build your own excitement? More than one dominatrix is wearing a pair of nipple clamps under her bustier to keep herself focused on her sniveling client. A famous domme author once referred to her extra-high heels as giving her a useful reservoir of irritability. I find it fascinating that in consensual BDSM, tops and bottoms and switches can all have a relationship with pain as a beloved friend and reward.

Some of my favorite play partners are tops who need a break. I am more than happy to anonymously provide a vacation for them at the other end of the whip. Every partner of mine is entitled to confidentiality. But because our community can be so stupid and judgmental about tops who get tired of always being the one to bark out the orders, I never even note the identities of these people in my journal. (As if anybody could ever read my handwriting.)

When a bottom whimpers and tells me they can't take any more, I have been known to whip out a pair of needles and pierce my own nipples. While they watch. If I can take it, I ask, why can't they?

And that's the perfect place to stop. Because there's only so much you can learn from reading a book. Go outside and play.

Submissive: A Personal Manifesto

Madison Young

I'm a mom. I'm a submissive. I'm a feminist. I struggle to write these words, finding myself in the greatest power-play dynamic of my life with a three-month-old infant who lies sleeping in my lap while I hunch over my laptop. She is a demanding dominant and I'm happy to serve her, to focus my energies around meeting her needs. I let the rest of the world slip away while she nurses from my breast. There is a sense of freedom in the experience, and I feel whole and complete in this energy exchange.

This feeling is not foreign to me. For the past six years, I've served her father as his submissive, lover, partner, and now the mother of his child. Ironically, my dedication to my child and my partner is what has made sitting down to write this essay the most challenging. My identity is complex—an interweaving of queer, masochist, rope slut, sex worker, control freak, loving partner and mother. Within these carefully constructed labels, in order to find my true self, I must give in. I must allow myself to be taken over, not just to fall deep down the rabbit hole but to jump, to fly, to dive in with knowledge.

To be the truest form of myself, I leap into a world of submission.

I am a multifaceted woman with dominant and submissive tendencies, a wide range of desires for sensation play and a need to play out different societal and animalistic roles in a safe environment with my partner. Sex is primal and has a magical, energetic rhythm to it—a pulse that you find in yourself or that passes between two or more persons. There are many ways to play with that pulse, that energy, both physically and psychologically. That pulse can be exchanged with great precision and control or it can knock you off your feet like a tidal wave.

Submission caters to my Virgo love of control and precision. Submission fulfills me, in the eroticism of lists and charts, in the satisfaction of completing a task. Submission penetrates me deeply with the pleasure of rules to obey and jobs well done. Submission is falling into a Zen space of control: constructing my being as an instrument of use and pleasure, allowing energy to flow through me, reprogramming the fibers of my being to reflect the desires of my Dominant. Submission is instinctively serving my Dominant, without effort, without being noticed or drawing attention. It's all about the details and serving another, not indulging in one's own sexual impulses. It's a delicious mix of cerebral and visceral sexuality, of control and instinct, of pleasure and selflessness.

To submit to my Dominant is to serve my Dominant, to pleasure him, to obey protocol, and to serve as a useful tool in the completion of tasks. Submitting is making his life and household run more smoothly as well as providing entertainment and pleasure. When I submit to my Dominant, I serve his erotic desires and fulfill mine; in practice, it might be as simple as walking behind my Dominant and to his right side, fetching tea and preparing it the way he likes it and never allowing his water glass to become less than half full at dinner. Or it could manifest as standing or kneeling rather than using a chair at dinner, a party or on the subway. These small acts of submission enveloped in our day-to-day activities can fill my being with erotic energy and a sense of connectedness and commitment to each other.

In our D/s relationship, we have a contract and basic protocol rules. We have different levels of protocol: basic everyday protocol, high protocol and, if need be, levels in between. One rule in our agreement states: "I will not use furniture, unless my Dominant has given me permission or if abiding by this rule would inconvenience or make others around me uncomfortable." (I would not stand or kneel at a restaurant or cafe if I was there without my Dominant or at a meeting where it would be inappropriate.) The rules in our contract help form the structure of our D/s relationship, and its creation is entirely unique to us. We understand that agreements can change based on the individuals' needs, which change over time, and we allow time on a regular basis to review our agreement to see what is working for each of us and what isn't. If something isn't working, we change it.

Sometimes, our D/s is incorporated into sex. I recall sitting at dinner at a four-star restaurant with my Sir. He ordered dessert for us, and as the waitress left the table he handed me a vibrator.

"Take this and get yourself off before our desert arrives, slut. And discreetly, my pet. I won't be needing any porn star theatrics. Subtlety is an art form after all."

"Yes, Sir."

I took the vibrator underneath the white tablecloth, under my dress, and up my slit, until it rested next to my clit. The buzzing vibrator was barely audible over the espresso machine in the back. I worked my way up to climax and quietly asked, "Sir, may I come?"

"Yes, you may come."

"Thank you, Sir."

Other times, D/s manifests when my Sir enforces an order, like denying me orgasms. I remember one business trip where I would be in Detroit for a week, and my Dominant ordered me not to masturbate during the trip. I was so incredibly turned on by the fact that I wasn't allowed to touch myself that I nearly came simply by the denial of my masturbation privilege.

If my Dominant and I are engaging in sadomasochism, I usually find myself in the role of a sensation-hungry lover or the submissive. If we are playing in an SM dynamic as lovers, I'm permitted to make eye contact. With each strike, we breathe together. It can be brutal and bloody, orgasmic and intimate all at the same time. If we're engaged in SM in a D/s protocol, I will not make eye contact and simply accept the energy of a whip or cane and allow it to flow through me without releasing moans of pleasure. I am only permitted to verbalize gratitude and respect, unless I am granted permission to come. In my role as a submissive, it's important for me to keep composure and always do my best to serve the needs of my Dominant, according to the terms of our D/s agreement, above my own impulses.

I was once performing in an on-camera scene with my Dominant and another woman. Her punishment for some indiscretion, which I now can't remember, was for her to watch as I took her caning for her. I knelt before my love, face forward, eyes focused ahead, arms behind my back, and took each strike with complete composure, only releasing breath and uttering a gracious "One. Thank you, Sir. Two. Thank you, Sir," until we reached twenty strikes. The girl stared at me crying and baffled by what she had just seen; she was puzzled to witness my intense composure during such a severe whipping and the deep level of submission I demonstrated.

In my relationship with my Dominant, he is my primary partner. But during the nearly six years of our relationship, I have petitioned for sexual and kinky relationships outside our own with agreed-upon partners. I once petitioned to be lent to a queer couple, a femme and a trans guy, for submissive service including domestic chores. The femme was the alpha Dominant in the relationship (both were dominant over me, but the femme Dominant was at the top of our hierarchy). After a decadent dinner in which I followed high-protocol standards (only speaking when spoken to, fetching jackets, pulling out chairs, opening the door) and serviced the couple sexually, I was ordered to the kitchen. A huge pile of dishes sat in the sink.

The two sat down at the kitchen table, post-sex and post-orgasm, a bit disheveled, sipping on tea in their boxers, lingerie and robes.

"Get to work, slut," Mistress ordered.

Naked and exhilarated in my submissive state, I got to work on the filthy dishes.

Mistress looked up drowsily from her tea and gifted me with her praise. "Such a good little submissive, slut. You are doing such a good job at those dishes. Jay, go get my whip."

Her partner returned with her whip and Mistress whipped my flesh, which was already marked from what had preceded in the bedroom that evening. As Mistress welted my skin with her whip, her fingers teasing my cunt every so often between strikes, and her partner sat at the kitchen table sipping his tea with a devilish grin, I felt absolute euphoric bliss in my service. It was one of those moments of clarity in which I feel that I am exactly where I am supposed to be, full of purpose and with an internal stillness that exists only in absolute surrender.

Submission is a gift of full surrender to another person. It's the removal of ego and self-indulgence. When I engage in a heavy D/s scene, I picture myself as a hollow cane of bamboo: I allow energy to flow through me, keeping complete focus and attention to my surroundings on my Dominant, without drawing attention to myself. It requires being aware of the rhythm of life around me, life in my scene, and how I play into that rhythm, that cacophony of sound. For example, the sound of a key in the door cues me to remove my panties and kneel into slave position with arms folded behind my back. The sound of the shower's running water instinctively starts me calculating how long that sound will last before Sir exits the shower and I enter with a fresh folded towel. The sound of the whistling kettle activates my anticipation to prepare Sir's tea. The whistling kettle, the shower water, and the key in the door are just as kinky to my auditory senses as the sound of the flogger coming into impact with my grateful flesh, the whisk of a cane, the yelp of other submissives, and the cries of orgasmic pleasure that surround us in public dungeons. It is humbling to serve, to give in, without ego, mindful and focused.

But as submissives, we are human. We will make mistakes, and if we choose to disobey or act in a disrespectful manner, we will be punished. The grace and dignity with which a submissive accepts a punishment is just as important as the manner in which you conduct yourself in daily service. It may be even more important.

I remember one instance when I allowed my emotions to get the better of me during a D/s scene with my Sir. Sir told me that because of a production schedule, he would have to work late on our anniversary, which was in a few weeks. This personal matter affected me as my Sir's lover, not as his submissive. I ran off from the scene in a huff and committed a cardinal sin in D/s: I took off my own collar. The collar is a symbol of dedication to our D/s relationship as well as a symbol of honor and respect reflecting my commitment to the BDSM community. In losing my composure and removing my collar, I was not only disrespecting my Sir but also acting as a disgrace to our community. Therefore my Sir decided that my punishment needed to be a public penance.

I treaded behind Sir in shame. I wished I could disappear and was thankful for the inviting darkness that the blindfold brought. I was led downstairs to a dungeon and placed on a suspended table; it was disorienting and difficult to balance on it without my sight. On all fours, presenting my ass, I awaited my punishment—rope biting around my chest, under my arms, pressed up against my rib cage, attempting to take over my breath and lead me into submission.

I felt floggers, paddles, hands, straps, belts, clamps, clothespins and mouths. I gently cooed, "Thank you, Sir," and "Thank you, Ma'am." I heard later that a line had formed; everyone wanted his or her turn. I changed positions, presenting my chest, my pussy, rotating to give onlookers a better view. I stood in difficult stress positions, squatting, balancing—all blindfolded. My head was spinning, chasing after the texture of voices in the room. I heard people negotiating with Sir. As he handed me over to the next participant, one politely asked me, "Could I go harder?"

"If it pleases you, Sir."

Another said, "You seem like such a good girl. What could you possibly have done to deserve this punishment?"

"I'm not at liberty to say, Sir. I'm sorry, Sir."

I followed the words like light, like butterflies. I let the sensation wipe through me at the hands of seasoned leathermen and Dominants and newbies who were shy and nervous. You would have thought they were the ones under the whip.

I could feel a community around me—young and old, SMers, experimenters and swingers. Each with a different stroke, a different touch. I was polite and grateful to them for taking part in my punishment.

Sir approached, whispering in my ear. "Just one more and I'll take you home."

"Thank you, Sir."

This swing was familiar. The cane struck my ass. I could feel the area of my flesh start to harden after repeated impact, and I could tell my skin had already started to bruise from hours of punishment. But I welcomed this touch. His touch.

"Count and show me you're sorry," he said.

"One. I'm sorry, Sir. Please, Sir, forgive me."

"Two. Sir, I'm so very sorry, Sir, I will be more mindful of my behavior, Sir." "Three. Sir, I'm sorry, Sir. I will only show the greatest of respect to us and our protocol, Sir."

I felt tired and broken. Worn down but at the same time fulfilled. I felt an unselfish pleasure from a job well done.

"You did good tonight, Maddie. I'm very proud of you. You made a lot of people very happy."

"Thank you, Sir."

Sex-positive feminism embraces the entire range of human sexuality and is based on the idea that sexual freedom is an essential component of women's freedom. BDSM is based on power and sensation play with a strong emphasis on communication and consent. I validate my own desires through the act of submission while simultaneously taking control of and embracing my sexuality. I have had to fight for my sexuality and identity, and I educate others around me about it. My personal has always been political. The aggressiveness with which I embrace my queer identity has translated to aggressiveness in claiming my submission.

Why is it fascinating and stimulating to engage in power exchange? We are breaking the rules. As queers, feminists, kinky persons and sexual outlaws, we have always broken the rules. We go outside designated sexual norms as we search for connection, community and fulfillment in our sexual lives and identities. Our sexual selves were not handed to us—we had to create them. We disassemble traditional power structures put in place by social norms only to reassemble them to use as our own sex toys.

Submissives are often strong and powerful women and men who wish to set aside or give their power to another person. Submissives are willing to make themselves vulnerable and open to experiences. We serve and give something back to both our community and to the one(s) we serve. Our service and education can result in both personal growth and community development. We submit to better the lives of others and, in doing so, our submission enriches our own lives.

In a fantasy world, Sir and I would exist 24/7 in an erotically charged nonstop BDSM scene. But this is reality—and thank goodness it is! It would be boring and not nearly as special to me if submission were a constant. It is difficult to fully appreciate the calm without a healthy amount of chaos. Besides, Sir and I lead very hectic lives, and between work and our newborn baby girl, it's not possible for us to maintain that dynamic of our relationship on a 24/7 basis. Instead we plan scenes or playdates. Or we find ways to work our D/s dynamic into our everyday lives. I welcome those moments like a breath of fresh air between diaper changes, breast-feedings, sexuality workshops and business meetings. After six years together, my partner and I have found what works for us. And this is what works for us. We are able to be loving partners to each other, passionate lovers, cuddle buddies, and coparents to our daughter, all as we engage in a Dominant/submissive scene.

Sometimes it's just for a moment, something as simple as Sir pulling my hair and bringing me to my knees before he leans down, kisses me on the crown of my head, and whispers, "I love you, slut." Or me saying, "I love you, Sir," before we head out to work. Sometimes that is all the time we have. But it only takes a moment. It's a subtle shift of power, an opening of my being, slipping into that quiet stillness of perfection and tranquillity. It's a state of Zen submission.

The space I go to when I'm in a position of submission is a meditative state. When painting or writing, I find myself going into a similar state. I have to step out of the way to give in to the creative energy. It's a state of pure connection, complete focus and the clarity discovered in letting go. I find it by riding waves of energy that flow through me with each impact from a heavy flogger or sting of a singletail. I find it in the precision and mindfulness with which I complete a task for my Sir. To sink into subspace, I allow my day, my life, my identity outside that moment, outside that scene, to slip into the background, and I offer myself as a vessel for the energy exchange between me and my Dominant.

Ghosts: All My Men Are Dead
Carol Queen

1

The ghost of Jack came back, sending me a spam email message many months after he had died. I cannot tell you how it felt to see his name pop up in that day's queue. I wasn't his primary lover, nor he mine. If anything I was down below tertiary, and we had not had any intimate time for ages—the sicker he got, the slimmer the chances became that we would ever again spend time in each other's arms. Partly this was just an artifact of illness, his body wasting and his energy ebbing. Our love was always a fuck-love, anyway; we'd never had enough time together for it to change into anything else. Partly it was that I felt it proper to move over to make room for his other lovers, the real ones, the ones who took him to the doctor and fed him well and helped him monitor his meds. If he had a single hard-on in the year before he died, I felt I should stand aside so it could point at them. Partly it was because of Robert: to have two men in my life disabled by illness was one too many, and I slowly closed to Jack to protect myself from the pain of it.

And partly it was because watching another man I loved waste and die felt impossible. I do not know how I could possibly have allowed myself to withdraw from him, from any of them, but as I saw time passing, and Jack getting worse and worse, my heart shut down. I still sent him love notes. I still held him when I saw him. I did not speak to him about it, did not let him in on my feelings, did not see a therapist, did not try for closure.

My heart still leaped, when he emailed me after he was dead.

If Jack had been failing because of an AIDS-related illness, they might have been able to help him. But the days when doctors eagerly try to diagnose mystery ailments in beautiful queer men are over. Now there are protocols. Now there are meds that will keep the men alive, changing their bodies into drug-mediated entities of different shape and ability—but alive—but Jack was sick with something else, something they never really diagnosed, so another one of the HIV-negative queer men, like Robert too, who dodged the bullet of the epidemic, was visited by illness just the same.

Now all my men—Robert the exception that proves the rule—are dead.

Death let Jack use his computer, though, and he sent me one email. I'm surprised there haven't been more—don't you think the Russian spammers might have discovered a way to harness the dead computer-savvy queers the way the Mormons consider the afterlife their own personal religious recruiting station? I wish he would write back to me, even if only to tell me about some other kind of software I can't live without. I trusted his recommendations about stuff like that when he was alive, too.

Most of my other men died before the Internet was a thing. They never write to me.

2

If I had come to San Francisco when I meant to—if I had run away to Haight-Ashbury when I was thirteen, as I dreamed of doing, if I had lit out right after high school and gotten here in the summer of 1974, if I had dropped out of college and joined Will when he moved to the city he called New Jerusalem in time to burn cars in the White Night riots of 1979, I would surely have caught this bullet. I'd have found my way to the commune in the Haight where the Cockettes lived. I'd have been an SM dyke with nowhere to play but the Catacombs, like Pat Califia. I'd have fucked bi men and fags like Cynthia Slater, the first woman I knew who did get HIV, and succumbed. If I had been playing beside her, with the same people, I might have been dead before Jack ever left his small city where he was the biggest scary queer they ever saw because, like all of us, his path inexorably led him to San Francisco.

If I had come to San Francisco when I really should have come, not just for a visit during Pride Week, but to claim my city and promise myself to her when she first called to me, I would have met David Lourea at the Bisexual Center in 1981. I'd have met Steven Brown at San Francisco Sex Information not in 1989, when I did meet him there, but sometime shortly after 1973. By the time I met Robert—who'd withdrawn from the baths years before HIV shut them down because he knew enough to see that steadily rising caseload of hepatitis boded no good—I might have been HIV-positive.

Before I'd have learned, in the early '80s, to be afraid, I'd have been unafraid, just like all the men whose sexual revolution in the 1970s inspired me from afar to try to understand from what cloth my own sexual revolution might be cut, a small-town dyke who really wanted to fuck practically every gay man she ever saw. Those men, finally unchained, had created their army of lovers, an army of lovers who could not fail: but who expected death to creep in along with the pleasure, along with the cocks-hard community-making? I came to San Francisco for the same reason they did: to fuck queer men, to make a home in New Jerusalem.

I have had the life I should have had in San Francisco, more or less. I came to partake of and foster the sexual revolution, and surely I have done some things that count for that. You should have seen us, in the early '90s, saying Fuck You to Death, making places for people to play safely, trying to sanitize these dangerous streets just enough to keep our people, the sex people, from dying. You should have felt how hot to the touch a naked cock could be when there was no sure way to keep someone alive if they got AIDS from the load that cock shot. What it meant to negotiate to be fluid-bonded when that bond had come to promise more than any ring: naked-cock sex was now coded to mean life or death, like the words the straight people said when they got married, but everyone knows they can get out of that if they want to.

I did not worship cock till I got to San Francisco, because nobody anywhere else I ever found people to fuck was proud enough of their cock, worshipful enough of other men's cocks, to override the fear and derision and tension that tempers desire with shame and dirt and mistrust. Most places, for most people, but in San Francisco? Here, fags sing hymns to cock, in Esperanto.

Besides, I was a dyke—a dyke who wanted to fuck fags, yes, but also a woman whose cultural context was so shot through with the bias of the binary that it scarcely let the possibility exist of real love between people whose bodies were different. Only when I could find that queer-on-queer love did it feel safe, feel like home, and open me to desire unsullied by the war-between-the-sexes taint that heterosexuality so often had.

And when I came home to that love, I found it tainted with something else.

3

I remember when I met Jack.

It was at a reading at 848 Community Space, and there he was, so sexy and magical in his long silver hair. Nothing else about him was elven; it was butch—his faded 501s fit tight as I slid a card into his pocket and told him to call if he wanted to be invited to a sex party. He cut his silvery hair later and I wondered if everyone else who loved and desired him felt as bereft as I did. Now I know that was just a foreshadowing of loss, one part of him slipping away, the rest finally ready to follow. All the men he did home-care for: their brothers are still alive, but because he did not have AIDS, in 2011 he died an old-school AIDS death.

I remember when I met Steven.

He stood in front of us at the SFSI training, tall, charismatic and funny, and told us about being a sex surrogate. He thought people came to him mainly to heal the part of their lives scarred by the absence of touch: We stroke our cats and dogs, he said, not each other. Steven lived with HIV for twenty years. He said that when you have a hundred things that get you off, giving up one or two of them wasn't such a loss as when those were the only things—naked cock in cunt or asshole, he meant—that could mean sex and pleasure.

I remember when I met Robert.

Tall, beautiful, the brightest eyes, describing himself as some older woman's Twinkie: that's how queers flag each other, with language and eye contact, and once we touched, I knew I'd do whatever it took to keep him in my life, and I have. "And we carried each other through it," he said, crying a little, as I told him I was writing about AIDS. The only thing that was powerful enough to overcome the times in which we lived was lust, and we had so much of it that for some years, we seemed to float above all the pain. Funny, this is not the narration of our love that I'd have constructed, but it's true: I wonder how many others, HIV-negative, met then and tried to create all the fuck-love in one place we felt our brothers being denied?

I remember when I met David.

Powerfully built and so very powerful in his spirit. His parents were Holocaust survivors; his sexuality became intertwined, even though he was a devoted sadomasochist, with the notion of *tikkun olam*, the care of the world. Only authentic sexuality *could*, in fact, carry us through the plague years—though David did not survive them. He once said that "Anything worth doing is worth doing poorly," a way to talk about harm reduction: every attempt, whether or not it was 100 percent successful, helped make things better, keep us safer, halt the virus more than it might have been halted if we just wilted in the face of it and did not try. David and I were like magnets, drawing each other close and then the polarities flipping, preventing our connection. For me it was the pure fear of loving someone with HIV—but I did love him, more than I was ever able to say or to show.

I remember when I met James.

A boyish, scruffy lawyer, the man who had made Oregon divest its investments from South Africa. On the heels of this success he joined the Willamette AIDS Council, where we worked together to try to create HIV awareness and advocacy from the ground up. He did not stay in Oregon long—he went to New York to work with the city's newly established AIDS Office as his T-cells dwindled and I tried to love him as lightly as I could— though we had spent his last month in Oregon necking like teenagers, he was a gay man and I was a lesbian (well, more or less) and our love for each other was like the Scarecrow's crossed arms: this way! That way!

He was not the only man who talked to me of his impending death without letting it become the weighty thing it really was, the millstone that would forever change the way my heart was able to beat. He did not tell me when it was time to come and see him to say good-bye. We beautiful, vital, sexual youths; we human thoroughbreds; I think we are ashamed to die.

4

Okay, so I keep telling you: I was a dyke.

That's only true insofar as "dyke" is an identity that can incorporate both a fierce love of, and identification with, women— plus in my case, a fierce love of, and identification with, fags. There really is no actual word for the thing that I was. But that is so true of so many of us; it's the reason we now just say "queer."

For a minute, after a youth full of bedpost-notching, the kind of frisky experimental fucking that teenagers do best, I tried to stay stable and lesbian. Well, that was never going to take, but I subsumed my desire for male bodies, my delight at sparring with men as a prelude to fucking them, into erotically charged friendships with gay men. One after the other, I created gay activist events and groups, my love for my coconspirators floating like oil on top of the water that was my connection with my women lovers. I might have gone on forever this way, my bisexuality living mostly in frantic masturbation sessions fueled by gay porn.

Until James. Until the gay man who should have pretended not to notice my crush instead kissed me good night until the windows of his Volkswagen steamed. Until the safely unattainable man turned out to be polymorphous enough—or enough in love with me too—to allow acknowledged, not silenced, erotic feeling to float in the air between us.

And how could a queer activist not take seriously the challenge and dilemma of forbidden love? We would never have wanted to be seen as any kind of straight, but the freedom to love is what our whole struggle was about. AIDS was the reason I went from lesbian to bisexual: that I might lose James made me see that the heart of my turn-on was pure love.

James opened the door to everything: queer men, queer sex, a newly (re)embraced bisexual identity, San Francisco...the person I have become. James wrote me a letter of recommendation when I applied to be the first woman working at an AIDS service organization—I didn't get the job, because it was still too soon for women to really be part of the change that would change everything, but James said this: "Carol is more comfortable with and for gay men than most gay men I know."

He did not live to read *The Leather Daddy and the Femme*, to watch *Bend Over Boyfriend*, to realize that I *did* walk through the door he opened. Many people offer us change, but only a few people change us as completely as James's love changed me.

And he set up, gracefully and inexorably, a pattern I have retained through all the men I've loved who are dead: a full stop regarding intimacy, sex, a relationship with a future. When that future spells death, neither I nor they ever try to keep me on the train.

5

Look at this city.

Go up to the East Bay hills or drive the frontage road in Berkeley. Take the ferry to Alcatraz or Angel Island. Emerge through the Waldo Tunnel for that fast, stunning shot of San Francisco framed by the tower of the Golden Gate Bridge, or go down to Fort Baker, where there's a Michelin-star restaurant now instead of an Army base. Drive through the Bay Bridge tunnel under Yerba Buena Island—do you always say, as Robert and I do, "Look, we *live* there"? Climb to the top of Potrero Hill or Bernal Heights. Take the ferry from Oakland or Marin. Look at the skyline, the hills, the bridges spanning away.

Or go to the top of Twin Peaks; from one side you can see the Pacific, the blocks of houses stretching off to the west and south. But from the other side, you look right down into the Castro. If you knew where to focus, you could pick out the top of the apartment house where Steven Brown lived, or any one of your old lovers—it probably doesn't happen anymore, but years ago, men who lived on the slopes of Twin Peaks could find a trick among all those apartments just by holding up a sign with their phone number written large enough to read from across the way, while they slowly worked their cocks on the balcony or at the kitchen window.

Every part of San Francisco has been touched by AIDS, but that swath of downslope, the valley below it and the hills that start to rise up again as you head south on Castro Street, that part was decimated as surely as if a neutron bomb had burned away the men who had lived there when I first came to San Francisco to visit Will during Pride Week in 1978. The next time I came, with my girlfriend Ellen, we walked the block from Market to Eighteenth Street after the parade, and it was so thick with men, bare-chested, Izod-shirted, tight-Levi'd, chaps-assed, nipple-ringed, drunk on Gay Pride and brotherhood, that we had to cling to each other's hands like swimmers fighting rapids to avoid being split apart and losing each other. It was the first time I had ever been surrounded by men with no feeling at all of fear. We were pressed in like a scrum of sardines, we were held securely between sweaty men, and I was so happy, I have no idea how I mustered the strength the next day to leave the city and go back to the mundane world. San Francisco *was* New Jerusalem; it was Oz.

That street streams with ghosts, day and night.

6

I didn't come here in the 1970s, because I was afraid. I was a small-town girl, and I remember when I believed San Francisco was such a big city. You have to be *ready* to do any new thing, unless the world forces you into it; otherwise, you grow into the time when what you could not do, you can. It's what maturation really means—this growing.

I did not think I could make a life for myself here. I swam in a small pond, the years ticked by, I waited to be ready to step into the world that I knew waited for me, and perhaps by doing so—though truly I cannot see it as anything but a failure of my character—I saved my own life.

We were not ready to lose our men. We were not ready to lose our friends and our lovers, and if the savage losses of the epidemic had happened to any single individual one of us, nearly all their friends gone, dying and then dying and still more dying, that one might have lost their mind with grief. Instead, it happened to all of us. The world forced us into it, and, drafted, watching each other die, some of us stayed alive and helped each other and waited for the future.

In the face of such a thing, fear means everything and it means nothing at all. Do you hide, move away, go straight? There must still be shell-shocked people everywhere who fled it. Do you sign up with Shanti or STOP AIDS or go walk somebody's dog? Or, like Robert and I did, throw a sex party, trying to deploy the only tool we trusted—and the one we ourselves needed—to help preserve sex in the face of all this fear?

All my dead men: I could not save them, can barely grieve them. Now that I finally found the courage to come here to find them, I am left with San Francisco: we are each widowed so many times.

Happy Hookers
Melissa Gira Grant

The following books were not published in 1972: *The Happy Secretary*, *The Happy Nurse*, *The Happy Napalm Manufacturer*, *The Happy President*, *The Happy Yippie*, *The Happy Feminist*. The memoir of a Manhattan madam was. *The Happy Hooker* climbed best–seller lists that year, selling over sixteen million copies.

When it reached their top five, the *New York Times* described the book as "liberally dosed with sex fantasies for the retarded." The woman who wrote them and lived them, Xaviera Hollander, became a folk hero. She remains the accidental figurehead of a class of women who may or may not have existed before she lived and wrote. Of course, they must have existed, but if they hadn't, say the critics of hooker happiness, we would have had to invent them.

Is prostitution so wicked a profession that it requires such myths?

We may remember the legend, but the particulars of the happy hooker story have faded. Hollander and the characters that grew up around her are correctly recalled as sexually omnivorous, but desire alone didn't make her successful as a prostitute. She realized that the sex trade is no underworld, that it is intimately entangled in city life, in all the ways in which we are economically interdependent. Hollander was famous for being able to sweep through the lobby of the Palace Hotel, unnoticed and undisturbed, on her way to an assignation, not because she didn't "look like" a working girl, but because she knew that too few people understood what a working girl really looked like.

In *The Happy Hooker Goes to Washington*, a 1977 film adapted from Hollander's memoir, a scene opens with Teletype bashing the screen with Woodward-and-Bernstein urgency. Flashlights sweep a darkened hall. Inside an unlocked office, a criminal scene is revealed: a senator embracing a prostitute. Hollander is called before Congress to testify. When the assembled panel interrogates her career, attacking her morals, she is first shameless, then spare but sharp in pointing out the unsurprising fact that these men are patrons of the very business they wish to blame for America's downfall. What's on trial in the film is ridiculous, but the questions are real. What value does a prostitute bring to society? Or is hooking really not so grandiose as all that? Could it be just another mostly tedious way to take ownership over something all too few of us are called before Congress to testify on—the conditions of our work?

"Did you know that 89 percent of the women in prostitution want to escape?" a young man told me on the first day of summer this year, as he protested in front of the offices of the *Village Voice*. He wanted me to understand that they are complicit in what he calls "modern-day slavery." The *Village Voice* has moved the bulk of the sex-related ads it publishes onto the website Backpage.com. This young man, the leader of an Evangelical Christian youth group, wanted to hasten the end of "sex slavery" by shutting Backpage.com down. What happens to the majority of people who advertise willingly on the site, who rely on it to draw an income? "The reality is," the man said to me, not knowing I had ever been a prostitute, "almost all of these women don't really want to be doing it."

Let's ask the people around here, I wanted to say to him: the construction workers who dug up the road behind us, the cabbies weaving around the construction site, the cops over there who have to babysit us, the Mister Softee guy pulling a double shift in the heat, the security guard outside a nearby bar, the woman working inside, the receptionist upstairs. The freelancers at the *Village Voice*. The guys at the copy shop who printed your flyers. The workers at the factory that made the water bottles you're handing out. Is it unfair to estimate that 89 percent of New Yorkers would rather not be doing what they have to do to make a living?

"True, many of the prostitution ads on Backpage are placed by adult women acting on their own without coercion," writes *New York Times* columnist and professional prostitute savior Nicholas Kristof. But, he continues, invoking the happy hooker trope, "they're not my concern." He would like us to join him in separating women into those who chose prostitution and those who were forced into it; those who view it as business and those who view it as exploitation; those who are workers and those who are victims; those who are irremediable and those who can be saved. These categories are too narrow. They fail to explain the reality of one woman's work, let alone a class of women's labor. In this scheme, a happy hooker is apparently unwavering in her love of fucking and will fuck anyone for the right price. She has no grievances, no politics.

But happy hookers, says Kristof, don't despair, this isn't about women like you—we don't really mean to put you out of work. Never mind that shutting down the businesses people in the sex trade depend on for safety and survival only exposes all of them to danger and poverty, no matter how much choice they have. Kristof and the Evangelicals outside the Village Voice succeed only in taking choices away from people who are unlikely to turn up outside the *New York Times,* demanding that Kristof's column be taken away from him.

Even if they did, with the platform he's built for himself as the true expert on sex workers' lives, men like Kristof can't be run out of town so easily. There's always another TED conference, another women's rights organization eager to hire his expertise. Kristof and those like him, who have made saving women from themselves their pet issue and vocation, are so fixated on the notion that almost no one would ever choose to sell sex that they miss the dull and daily choices that all working people face in the course of making a living. Kristof himself makes good money at this, but to consider sex workers' equally important economic survival is inconvenient for him.

This business of debating sex workers' choices and whether or not they have them has only become more profitable under what sociologist Elizabeth Bernstein terms "post-industrial prostitution." After the vigilant antiprostitution campaigns of the last century, which targeted red-light districts and street-based prostitution, sex work has moved mostly indoors, into private apartments and gentlemen's clubs, facilitated by the Internet and mobile phones.

The sex economy exists in symbiosis with the leisure economy: personal services, luxury hotels, all increasingly anonymous and invisible. At the same time, more young people find themselves without a safety net, dependent on informal economies. Sex work now isn't a lifestyle; it's a gig, one of many you can select from a venue like Backpage or Craigslist.

Recall the favored slogan of prostitution prohibitionists that on the Internet, they could buy a sofa and "a girl." It's not the potential purchase of a person that's so outrageous; it's the proximity of that person to the legitimate market. Bernstein calls these "slippery borders," and asks us to observe the feelings provoked by them, and how they are transferred. Anxieties about slippery market borders become "anxieties about slippery moral borders," which are played out on the bodies of sex workers.

The anxiety is that sex work may be legitimate after all. In a sense, the prohibitionists are correct: people who might have never gotten into the sex trade before can and are. Fighting what they call "the normalizing of prostitution" is the focus of anti–sex work feminists. In this view, one happy hooker is a threat to all women everywhere.

"It's sad," said the speaker from the women's-rights NGO Equality Now in protest outside the *Village Voice*. She directed her remarks at the cluster of sex workers who had turned out in counterprotest. "Backpage is able to be a pimp. They're so normalizing this behavior that a group of Backpage advertisers have come out today to oppose us." So a prostitute's dissent is only possible if, as they understand prostitution itself, she was forced into it.

"Why did it take so long for the women's movement to genuinely consider the needs of whores, of women in the sex trades?" asks working-class queer organizer and ex-hooker Amber L. Hollibaugh, in her book *My Dangerous Desires*. "Maybe because it's hard to listen to—I mean really pay attention to—a woman who, without other options, could easily be cleaning your toilet? Maybe because it's intolerable to listen to the point of view of a woman who makes her living sucking off your husband?"

Hollibaugh points to this most difficult place, this politics of feelings performed by some feminists, in absence of solidarity. They imagine how prostitution must feel, and how that in turn makes them feel, despite all the real-life prostitutes standing in front of them to dispute them.

It didn't used to be that people opposed to prostitution could only get away with it by insisting that "happy" prostitutes didn't really exist. From *Gilgamesh* to the Gold Rush days, right up until Ms. Hollander's time, being a whore was reason enough for someone to demand you be driven out of town. Contemporary prostitution prohibitionists consider the new reality, in which they deny the existence of anyone with agency in prostitution, a form of victory for women. We aren't ruined now. We're victims.

Perhaps what they fear most of all is that prostitutes could be happy: that what we've been told is the worst thing we can do to ourselves is not the worst, or even among the worst. What marks us as fallen—whether from feminism or Christ or capital—is any suggestion that prostitution did not ruin us and that we can deliver that news ourselves.

Christian Conservatives vs. Sex: The Long War Over Reproductive Freedom

Rob Boston

On November 1, 1961, Estelle Griswold and Dr. Charles Lee Buxton did something radical: they opened a clinic in New Haven, Connecticut, to dispense birth control information.

Nine days later, police raided the clinic and arrested Griswold, executive director of the Planned Parenthood League of Connecticut, and Buxton, chairman of the obstetrics department at Yale Medical School.

Buxton and Griswold weren't surprised. In fact, they had been expecting to be arrested all along. Their decision to open a birth control clinic in New Haven was a deliberately provocative act, designed to test a law originally passed in Connecticut in 1879 that banned artificial forms of contraceptives in the state for everyone—even married couples.

Connecticut's anti–birth control statute was only being sporadically enforced at the time, and some types of birth control were available in drugstores. But Buxton and Griswold believed that as long as the law was in place, access to contraceptives wasn't secure.

Sure enough, when they opened their facility, conservative religious leaders went on the warpath. The state's politically powerful Roman Catholic hierarchy demanded action, leading to the raid on the clinic.

Buxton and Griswold went to court. They lost at every level in Connecticut state courts, including before the state supreme court. But in 1965, the U.S. Supreme Court reversed the pair's convictions and ruled 7-2 in Griswold v. Connecticut that the law was unconstitutional.

Citing "the zone of privacy created by several fundamental constitutional guarantees," Justice William O. Douglas observed, "Would we allow the police to search the sacred precincts of marital bedrooms for telltale signs of the use of contraceptives? The very idea is repulsive to the notions of privacy surrounding the marriage relationship. We deal with a right of privacy older than the Bill of Rights...."

Five years earlier, the U.S. Food and Drug Administration granted approval for sale to the public of the first oral contraceptive. Within two years, more than a million American women were on "the Pill." The number escalated as refinements continued in years to come.

Today, most Americans believe access to contraceptives is secure; younger Americans may not even know about the case involving Buxton and Griswold.

But as recent events have shown, birth control—although regarded as noncontroversial and indeed necessary by most Americans—remains a political flashpoint. When President Barack Obama announced earlier this year that most employers, including religiously affiliated institutions such as hospitals, universities and social service agencies, would have to contract with insurance companies that would make contraceptives available to employees who want them, conservative religious groups were quick to stir up opposition.

The Catholic hierarchy insisted that the mandate to include contraceptives would violate religious liberty—even though under the policy their institutions are not required to directly pay for it.

The bishops then upped their demands and began pressing for federal legislation that would give any employer (even in non-religious settings) the right to exclude birth control coverage in health-care plans if it offended his or her religious beliefs—a move, critics said, that could potentially deny or greatly restrict access to millions of Americans.

In the wake of the national controversy, lawmakers in several states began pushing legislation that would have the effect of restricting access to birth control. One of the more extreme measures surfaced in Arizona, where a bill that would have allowed any employer with religious objections to deny contraceptive coverage passed the state House of Representatives.

The measure, which stalled in the state Senate only after a public outcry, would allow a woman access to the Pill for medical reasons but only after she proved to her employer that she wasn't using it for birth control, a provision opponents called patronizing and a violation of medical privacy.

The aggressive nature of the joint legislative and sectarian assault on contraceptives dismayed many birth control advocates.

"I am completely shocked that contraception is being made to seem as if it's a controversial issue," said the Rev. Debra W. Haffner, president of the Religious Institute, a Connecticut-based group that examines the intersection of theology and human sexuality. "The fact is, ninety percent of heterosexual, sexually active adults use contraception. More than nine in ten American adults support the availability of contraception."

Haffner noted that support for this issue used to be bipartisan. As a member of the House of Representatives during the 1970s, future president George H.W. Bush championed family planning initiatives, and President Ronald W. Reagan signed them into law during the 1980s.

Why the change now?

"I think what is going on now has virtually nothing to do with contraception," Haffner, a Unitarian Universalist minister, told *Church & State*. "It has to do with both the Catholic bishops and the extreme evangelical right looking for new wedge issues to continue to try to impose their beliefs about sexuality on the general public. I believe that the Catholic bishops are trying to do through legislation what they've been unable to do from their pulpits, which is influence the way their congregants enjoy their sexuality."

She added that many conservative religions maintain that sex exists only for procreation, a view they seek to have reflected in secular law.

"The Pill enabled people through technology to enjoy sexual pleasure without the possibility of reproduction, separating sexual behavior from procreation," Haffner said. "In today's world, it's not just a pill but patches and rings and implants and lots of modern methods of sterilization that are effective. There's an affirmation of sexuality that now exists that to a very small group of people is very frightening."

Although, as Haffner points out, birth control comes in many forms, most of the discussion centers around oral medication that has become so ubiquitous it is called simply "the Pill."

The Pill remains the most popular form of contraceptive in America. In 2010, the Centers for Disease Control and Prevention reported that 82 percent of all women who had sex with men reported that they had been on the Pill at some point in their lives. Nationwide, about eleven million women of childbearing age were estimated to be on the Pill at that time.

The Pill, condoms, intrauterine devices, permanent sterilization and other forms of birth control have become so common and popular that it's easy for people today to forget how hard they once were to get. Easy access to contraceptives is the exception in America. For most of our history, a potent combination of church and state blocked not only access to birth control but access to information about birth control. Amazingly, some forces today want to go back to those days.

For most of human history, birth control was unreliable, erratic and often dangerous to women. Some women used wool, cotton, linen and other materials to block the cervix. Various potions were also said to function as spermicide, although much of this was folklore. (One early preparation consisted of crocodile dung and honey.)

Early condoms, often made of linen or animal bladders, were used during the Roman Empire and into the Middle Ages. For the hundreds of years that followed, not many other options were available.

The discovery of the vulcanization of rubber by Charles Goodyear, a process that was patented in 1844, led to the introduction of rubber condoms in America. Early rubber condoms were thick, brittle and often unreliable, but by 1920 latex condoms had been invented, and their use quickly caught on.

But there were also forces determined to prevent the widespread use of contraceptives of any kind in America. Self-appointed anti-vice crusaders joined forces with religious leaders to crack down on material deemed "obscene"—and that included even information of a clinical nature about birth control.

Most famously, Anthony Comstock, a devout Congregationalist in New York, secured passage of a federal law that allowed the Post Office to ban "lewd" and "lascivious" material. This included not only books and magazines dealing with sexual topics but contraceptives and information about them.

Material circulated secretly through an underground, and doctors often signaled their willingness to discuss the topic of birth control (and sexually transmitted diseases) in advertisements using code words such as "private complaints" or "delicate matters."

Attempts to bring the discussion of birth control into the open were quickly squashed. This continued well into the twentieth century. New England states with strong Catholic traditions were hotbeds of anti–birth control activism.

New England today is often viewed as a bastion of political liberalism, but for many years the region languished under heavy-handed forms of clerical censorship. Catholic clergy and their allies were also successful in curbing access to contraception.

Americans United, which was founded in 1947, quickly recognized that the battle over birth control had strong church–state implications. Many Americans, the organization noted, wanted to use contraceptives but were stymied because they lived in states where clerical interference made that impossible.

The pages of *Church & State* in the late 1940s, '50s and '60s are studded with stories about often-successful attempts to block access to birth control, mainly by Catholic leaders and their allies working in concert with government officials.

In 1949, four doctors were fired from Farren Memorial Hospital in Greenfield, Massachusetts, because they refused to stop discussing birth control with patients who had requested the information. Hospital officials offered to reinstate the doctors if they would publicly admit they were wrong, vow to stop discussing the issue and promise not to contradict Catholic views again. The four refused.

Three years later, a flap erupted in Massachusetts over whether doctors should have the legal right to discuss birth control with patients. State law at the time prohibited doctors from providing information on the topic even if patients asked about it.

Planned Parenthood launched a drive to repeal the law and secured more than eighty thousand signatures on petitions, but Catholic Church leaders raised so many objections that the legislature was cowed and refused to act.

Nearly one thousand miles to the west, birth control advocates in Chicago announced plans in 1960 to add information about contraceptives at a clinic that served a largely low-income population. Pressure from the Catholic hierarchy soon scuttled the plan, a result officials at Planned Parenthood deemed "reprehensible."

The controversy even reached overseas. In 1949, U.S. military forces in occupied Japan rescinded an invitation that had been extended to birth control advocate Margaret Sanger. Sanger had been invited to the country, which was still under American control following World War II, by Japanese civic organizations, but Catholic groups raised so many objections that Sanger was denied the necessary military clearance.

As late as 1970, William R. Baird, a birth control advocate in New York, was being harassed by police for giving public lectures on contraceptives and abortion. In 1967, Baird was arrested in Boston after he distributed contraceptive foam to students during a lecture at Boston University. Baird was charged with violating a state "chastity" law prohibiting the distribution of birth control to unmarried persons, a felony punishable by ten years in prison.

His conviction was voided by the Supreme Court in 1972 in Eisenstadt v. Baird, a ruling that extended the right to use birth control to unmarried couples.

Baird, now eighty years old, still lectures about reproductive justice. He told *Church & State* that he was at first reluctant to challenge the Massachusetts law.

"My initial reaction when I saw the penalty," he recalls, "was, 'I have four kids. I can't afford to be in prison for ten years.'"

Baird changed his mind after students pleaded with him to come.

"I thought of a young woman I once saw in a hospital who died from an illegal abortion," Baird said. "I was so absolutely outraged that a fellow human being was dying in front of me because she could not legally have birth control."

By this time, the issue was becoming a little less volatile in religious circles because many Protestant churches had accepted birth control and told their congregants that its use was not a sin. But the Catholic hierarchy remained entrenched.

In 1963, Pope John XXIII formed a commission to study the issue. The pope died before the commission could complete its work, and its members later recommended to Pope Paul VI that the church's ban on artificial contraceptives be lifted. Church hardliners immediately fired back with their own report. In 1968, Pope Paul sided with the hardliners and issued *Humanae Vitae,* an encyclical that affirmed the church's ban on all forms of artificial contraception.

As a practical matter, the ban has proved impossible for the church to enforce, and numerous studies have shown that sexually active Catholics rely on birth control at the same rate as non-Catholics. Many Catholic women, like their non-Catholic counterparts, also use the pill for medical reasons, such as to shrink ovarian cysts, to manage endometriosis or lessen menstrual cramps.

Why, after so many years of struggle, is birth control suddenly an issue again?

One reason is that some members of the Catholic hierarchy and the Religious Right have never accepted the premise of the 1965 Griswold ruling. The right to privacy outlined there appeared again in 1973's Roe v. Wade, which legalized abortion in the United States. Antiabortion church leaders blasted Roe—and some didn't hesitate to trace its origins back to Griswold.

TV preacher Pat Robertson has several times made the connection explicit. Addressing his political group, the Christian Coalition, in 1997, Robertson blasted Griswold as "made up out of whole cloth."

Said Robertson of the ruling, "I want to see it abolished."

According to ultraconservative religious leaders, the right to privacy that undergirds Griswold has spawned a raft of problems. In 2003, for example, the Supreme Court struck down a Texas law criminalizing consensual same-sex relationships. In its Lawrence v. Texas decision, the high court cited both Griswold and Eisenstadt.

But there is a deeper reason: many religious fundamentalists have never made peace with the social and cultural changes that the Pill—a safe, effective and affordable form of birth control— brought about.

The Pill has been called the most important invention of the twentieth century, and while some believe that designation is overblown—nuclear weapons, the computer and the World Wide

Web are also contenders—there's no denying its powerful cultural impact.

The Economist put it well in a special issue published on the brink of the twenty-first century: "[B]efore the 1950s the unpredictability of the arrival of children meant that the rights of many women were more theoretical than actual," observed the publication. "The Pill really did give a woman the right to choose. And though the consequences of that choice are still working themselves out, as both men and women adjust to the new reality, one difference between the passing millennium and those to come is clear: women have taken a giant step towards their rightful position of equal partnership with men. Technology really is liberation."

Fundamentalist Protestants and the male-only Catholic hierarchy, who have never been known for their support of women's rights, have sought ways to reverse that giant step. Laws banning contraceptives outright are unlikely to win legislative approval in the modern era. But sectarian opponents of birth control don't have to go that far to curb access. If their "religious freedom" argument carries the day, millions of American men and women may wake up to find out their health care plans no longer pay for birth control pills, IUDs, sterilization operations and other methods— and that, essentially, their ability to use birth control hinges on their employers' religious beliefs.

Advocates for contraception say Americans should not be sanguine about this issue.

"The American public—both men and women, straight and LGBT, both young and post-reproductive age—need to be very frightened about the attacks on reproductive health," Haffner said. "The current attack on whether contraception will be included in health care reform is actually only a small piece of what's happening across the country to effectively turn back people's sexual rights.

"Once the government is able to deny the right to privacy," she continued, "they can legislate against anyone's sex life. All of our ability to make our own informed decisions about our sex lives becomes in jeopardy."

Americans United Executive Director Barry W. Lynn agrees. Lynn's activism in this area may run in his blood: he remembers a story his mother told him about how as a young woman she was kicked out of a coal mining town in eastern Pennsylvania for distributing birth control information.

"Access to affordable, effective and safe birth control was achieved only by standing up to entrenched sectarian interests who were determined to bend the law to their oppressive dogma," Lynn said. "We broke their grip, and we simply can't go back now."

Porn Defends the Money Shot

Dennis Romero

It's the staple of porn and an element of Americana so pervasive that it has become a term to describe any crescendo in pop culture, from a game-winning basket by Kobe Bryant to an emphatic punch line by Sarah Palin.

More than twenty years ago Jeff Koons made his soon-to-be wife, porn star La Cicciolina, the star of his explicit *Made in Heaven* series of huge photo portraits, which, in part, glorified and immortalized the money shot, giving it a place even in the world of haute art.

Almost everything in adult video leads up to the final "pop," as those in the business call the visual release of semen. But most of the rest of the time is spent setting up shots and adjusting body parts for the perfect lead-up. Behind the scenes, it actually can be tedious to witness. And there's no fast-forward.

Watching *Star Wars XXX: A Porn Parody* (released in February

2012) being made this summer was certainly anticlimactic. Billed as the most expensive adult film ever, its production was as professional and deliberate as any big-budget Hollywood project: take after take, flubbed lines, megaphone instructions to the cast, minutes if not hours of breaks to set up shots, makeup, wardrobe, extras walking around in storm trooper costumes.

Even a furry Chewbacca look-alike paced the set—a stuffy warehouse just west of the Los Angeles River downtown—letting out the occasional, wistful growl.

And Princess Leia. Oh, Princess Leia—played by Vivid Entertainment's newest contract star, Allie Haze. If not for Haze strutting around the set, her hair in trademark buns, her obscene curves visible beneath a sheer white gown, it all would have been an absolute bore.

In the last few years, the rise of free online porn—content-rich sites that tease viewers to subscribe for more—and pay-site juggernauts like Brazzers have put the L.A.-based adult-video industry against the ropes. Its answer, in part, has been the high-dollar parody, designed to attract ComicCon nerds, science fiction fans and other pop culture aficionados who must collect everything within their target oeuvre.

On the eve of the fortieth anniversary of porn's introduction to the mainstream via *Deep Throat* and *Behind the Green Door*, it might be too little, too late.

"That's the main reason for the success of my movies—because I went after a different demographic," *Star Wars XXX* director Axel Braun tells the *Weekly* on set. "I'm not going after fans of porn; I'm going after fans of the original source material."

Braun's films, in partnership with Vivid, the industry's largest studio, have been blockbusters at a time when—as with mainstream studios, record labels and newspapers—online consumption is draining profits. Porn parodies (*Elvis XXX*, *Spider-Man XXX*) are a rare bright spot in an industry that has seen its bottom line rocked.

Filmmaker and industry activist Michael Whiteacre says porn star unemployment is high, with performers "working a lot less and getting paid a lot less. The money is just not there for these girls."

And so many adult actors, particularly the women, are devolving to work as "escorts," a kinder term for prostitutes. Former performer Gina Rodriguez says that if the girls last one year in porn movies—most last only three to six months—they get hooked on the relatively big money and gravitate toward prostitution when the film producers seek fresh new faces and bodies.

"It's a money trap," Rodriguez says. "They take in the eighteen-, nineteen-year-olds, and within a year they'll be into escorting."

In the past, a porn star taking money for off-camera work might not be a big deal. But the straight-porn biz is under attack for its general refusal to use condoms—even on uber-mainstream sets like *Star Wars XXX*, where producers say prophylactics are optional, but nobody uses them. Porn leaders insist that once-a-month testing of performers keeps the L.A.-based pool of workers safe from the likes of HIV.

But when straight-porn actors take side gigs as prostitutes to make a living, having sex with strangers off-set, that changes everything. They're quietly going outside the safe pool. Some are almost assuredly not using condoms, then returning to local porn sets—two hundred porn productions pull permits every month in the City of Los Angeles alone—without a word.

The L.A.-based AIDS Healthcare Foundation (AHF) is on a

mission to get state and local authorities to enforce condoms on set. On the surface, it's not a bad idea, especially if porn stars free-lance as hookers.

But here's the key stumbling block: that would also mean the end of the industry's bread and butter—the sacred money shot, shooting semen and all. Industry leaders are fighting tooth and nail against condoms. Even a relatively mainstream filmmaker like Braun says condoms would push production out of state be-cause the mostly male viewers just don't want to see films where a key component is sheathed in latex.

"We're selling a fantasy," he says, adding later: "Think about it. If you make something illegal that has so much demand, you're going to send it underground. You send it underground, you're going to have people not getting tested anymore.

"I don't think it's the right approach."

AIDS Healthcare Foundation seized on news in August of an-other HIV scare in porn. After a performer in Miami had an initial positive test from a medical clinic for the virus that causes AIDS, a weeklong shutdown of porn production from coast to coast in early September ensued, affecting scores of major and minor productions.

Luckily for the titans of this industry, it turned out to be a false positive. They got back to work, but not before accusing AIDS Healthcare Foundation and its leader, Michael Weinstein, of being overzealous in their attacks against the porn industry and its wholesomely named lobbying group, the Free Speech Coalition.

Weinstein accused the industry of "a full-scale cover-up" in its reaction to the HIV scare, noting that it took nearly a week for the public to find out whether the unnamed porn actor actually was positive and that "the results of any confirmatory tests should already be available" before that.

Because Free Speech Coalition took the lead in publicly explaining the Miami case, Weinstein criticized the group, telling reporters it "is not qualified to investigate a public health outbreak of this kind." However, FSC's leaders dismiss his criticism.

Free Speech Coalition and Manwin, the porn company that employed the male performer, both called for Weinstein to "retract" his allegations. It has been, to be sure, a war of words.

Porn's leaders seem to march in lockstep in accusing AHF and Weinstein of having a profit motive: many of them allege the health care group wants to take over testing for porn, wants a potentially lucrative contract for inspecting sets and even wants to get into the highly competitive business of producing condoms—which it would sell to the adult-video business.

"This is about money," says filmmaker Whiteacre.

Weinstein retorts: "We're not interested in doing testing for the porn industry. We already have our own brand of condoms, which we give out for free."

AHF bills itself as "the nation's largest provider of HIV/AIDS medical care," and it had assets of eighteen million dollars in 2010. Condoms and porn first appeared on its map in 2004, when a Los Angeles performer named Darren James contracted HIV, apparently during a trip to Brazil, where he worked and exposed twelve female performers to the possibility of HIV-positive status.

Ironically, back then, some of the bigger producers like Vivid, which focused on softer-core pay-per-view sales at major hotel chains, were condom-mandatory companies by choice, so condoms were used for everything but oral sex. But tastes got raunchier, even in otherwise buttoned-up hotels that cater to business travelers, and the condoms came off for good. After the 2004 outbreak (at least three women who worked with James after he returned to L.A. from Brazil tested positive for HIV), AHF took an official stance in favor of mandatory condoms. In 2009 the health care group started to lobby actively for the rule.

That's when the group discovered that using condoms during porn shoots was already required under federal law—albeit a law everyone had ignored.

Senior officials at the California Division of Occupational Safety and Health (Cal-OSHA) say that its interpretation of federal law prohibiting employees from being exposed to blood-borne pathogens (blood, semen and the like) means that condoms are indeed required on set.

And so, after AIDS Healthcare Foundation began filing complaints against companies like Larry Flynt's Hustler video empire, carting boxes of DVDs depicting condom-free sex to the offices of Cal-OSHA, the workplace-safety division started levying fines on a piecemeal basis.

Flynt's company was hit last March with fourteen thousand dollars worth of fines for failing to require its actors to use condoms. The multimillion-dollar enterprise didn't even feel the tiny sting. Flynt practically yawned, declaring he wouldn't require condoms at Hustler productions.

Cal-OSHA officials admit to *LA Weekly* that resources for enforcing the federal blood-borne pathogens law are scarce during this era of multibillion-dollar state deficits. Deborah Gold, Cal-OSHA senior safety engineer, said late last year, "We realize that strong, consistent enforcement is imperative to our program. We're doing what we can within our resources."

Cal-OSHA lead counsel Amy Martin refuted that stance in a recent interview. She says the state is actively investigating possible on-set violations but reveals that the state is focused on reacting to complaints—not on digging up problems through surprise checks. The lack of "resources has not prevented us from opening inspections based on complaints," she says.

AHF has pleaded with the City of Los Angeles and the L.A. County Department of Public Health to come down on productions that don't require condoms. A memo from the office of City Attorney Carmen Trutanich in April indicated that condom use was required under L.A.'s permitting process, noting, "California Code of Regulations Section 5193 [requires] employees exposed to blood-borne pathogens to wear protective gear. In the event any terms of the permit are violated during the permitted activity, LAPD has the discretion to revoke the permit."

But that's not happening, even as more and more porn actors in Southern California turn to prostitution, dragging unknown pathogens into the acting pool, thanks to the recession and the severe economic hit from free online porn.

Trutanich's office informed the City Council that "it's doubtful" Los Angeles can "actively enforce" condom use on set. It seems that lack of resources is to blame: imagine the Los Angeles Police Department acting as prophylactic police. County health chief Jonathan Fielding said the same—that regulating the adult industry's workplaces is a state duty.

The industry has argued that the blood-borne pathogen rule doesn't apply to it, that it was intended to cover medical clinics, and that requiring such possible "protective gear" as latex gloves, goggles and face masks on set would be absurd—but state officials say that's not what the law requires.

"The idea they would consider applying a rule created for medical clinics and emergency rooms to an adult production— it's hard to choose from the variety of insulting words: asinine, mindless, inappropriate," says attorney Jeffrey Douglas, chair of

FSC's board of directors. "If it were in effect, dental dams would be mandatory and everybody would have to wear rubber gloves. Everyone would have to be more closely protected than a dentist working on your mouth."

Some porn insiders also note that mixed martial arts fighters (of the Ultimate Fighting Championship variety) are often exposed to blood during bouts that are sanctioned by the state of California.

Again, the state responds that its investigators focus on complaints, not on proactively trying to unearth exposure to pathogens. Cal-OSHA's Martin says that if the agency received complaints about blood exposure in "the octagon"—the eight-sided enclosure where UFC competitors fight—the state agency would investigate and issue citations where necessary.

So far, the industry's major straight-porn producers (gay porn largely employs condoms for anal sex but often allows the money shot in other cases) have ignored the federal mandate. Cal-OSHA, at the behest of AIDS Healthcare Foundation, has been working on a specific rule that would cover adult video in California—specifically mentioning condoms and the industry instead of relying on federal law that might or might not have been intended for medical facilities.

The new rule could be taken up by Cal-OSHA's standards board by the end of 2011—and that will set off a fury in the already hammered porn industry. Nobody knows if it will contain fines significantly bigger than the fourteen thousand dollar fine on Flynt, which he laughed off.

Cal-OSHA attorney Martin tells the *Weekly* there's no way to know if the proposed new rule, designed to force mandatory condom use squarely upon adult-video makers, would actually change the way the business behaves.

"I don't know," she says, pausing. "Hopefully they'll comply with the law."

At a June meeting to discuss the proposed rule in an auditorium at a state building in downtown L.A., about seventy performers showed up, mostly to protest. You've never seen such tight jeans and structurally sound body parts in a Caltrans facility.

During the hearing a female performer stood up and said, "You guys are discussing what I need to do with my own body."

It's a point frequently argued by some of the women of porn: this is a privacy issue, just like the right to abortion. "I don't know how they can tell us what I can and can't put in my body," Haze says while on the set of *Star Wars XXX*. "It's a choice."

At summer's Adultcon convention downtown, porn star Trinity St. Clair was wearing a schoolgirl uniform, inspiring a gray-haired man to say, "She looks barely old enough," before he posed for a picture with St. Clair. But talk turned more serious when she said, "We get to decide what we want to do as women. It's kind of like abortion and those rights."

Perhaps the most interesting argument against using condoms in porn movies comes from Roger Jon Diamond, a Santa Monica attorney who has been involved for many years in defending strip clubs and adult businesses. He cites freedom of speech.

"I would say such a rule would interfere with the First Amendment right of the producer and director to create a product," he says. "I don't think the state has the authority to do that. It would be a public health issue versus a freedom-of-expression issue. If it interfered with the artistic nature of the movie, I think there would be a First Amendment argument. But, in terms of politics, I don't think the industry wants to take on this battle."

It would take serious time, dollars and legal might for the adult biz to fight for its right to the money shot as a form of artistic expression. But some in the industry are gung-ho. Mandatory condoms, says porn star and activist Nina Hartley, would be "prior restraint on speech."

The death of John Holmes (the inspiration for Mark Wahlberg's character in *Boogie Nights*) in 1988 was attributed to AIDS, and many blamed his "crossover" work in gay film and his alleged drug use.

Denial is a river that overflows in the industry of smut, and Holmes was seen by many performers as a victim of his own lifestyle choices. It wasn't until 1993, when another HIV outbreak hit the industry, that porn began to think seriously about how to confront the virus and other STDs, says William Margold, an industry veteran and gadfly who has worked as a writer, actor and filmmaker since the early 1970s.

In 1998 industry insider and former porn star Sharon Mitchell launched the Adult Industry Medical Healthcare Foundation (AIM), a nonprofit where performers could get tested and treated. By the next decade, it was the epicenter of the industry's official testing protocol. Performers working for major production companies such as Vivid, Evil Angel and even the more online-focused Manwin are tested monthly and must show proof of negative HIV results when they arrive on set.

In recent years AIM even began posting the results of porn stars' tests on a restricted website, which producers could check to see if an actor was good to perform.

That all changed last spring, when a website called PornWikiLeaks put online, for the world to see, performers' medical records, apparently culled from AIM's database and sometimes matched with addresses that are federally required to ensure movie performers aren't underage.

At about the same time, AIDS Healthcare Foundation was filing complaints against the Adult Industry Medical Healthcare Foundation as part of its mission to get condoms required in porn. In AHF's view, testing service AIM was the new enabler in the industry's denial about condoms.

On one front, AHF alleged that AIM was violating performers' federal privacy rights by making their test results available online to producers; on another it said AIM wasn't properly registered as a clinic, which was true.

Legal action by AHF ultimately toppled AIM last May, when the organization closed its doors. The Free Speech Coalition stepped in with a replacement system called the Adult Production Health and Safety Service, which promised to honor privacy while administering the once-a-month testing protocol.

The industry argues that its testing system works by quickly alerting it to new HIV cases, leading to shutdowns of production, preventing HIV from spreading on set.

Of the ten HIV cases in the porn industry that both the AHF and the Free Speech Coalition agree have cropped up since 2005, the industry says nearly all were contracted off-set, the implication being that many of the original virus carriers didn't work in the industry. FSC chair Douglas says, "In all of the tens of thousands of unprotected sex acts [since 2005], there is only one documented occasion where someone transmitted HIV on the set. That's a regret. It should never have happened."

STD rates for performers are "much lower" than those of the general population, says FSC executive director Diane Duke. Such numbers are hard to calculate, however, because porn's population of workers is transient and changes by the month, a fact Johns Hopkins M.D. Lawrence S. Mayer noted in an industry-commissioned report that debunks studies claiming high STD rates in adult video, which he called "without basis in science."

One of the industry's more unsavory arguments against using condoms is that some of its HIV cases occurred when male straight-porn actors engaged in unprotected "crossover" work in gay porn, or had relations with gay men in their personal lives.

In 2004, when James contracted HIV after his visit to South America, Ron Jeremy suggested with a metaphorical wink to this author that there are a lot of beautiful women in Brazil, "and some of them have dicks."

Derrick Burts, the performer who tested HIV-positive in 2010, was quickly outed by industry insiders as not only a crossover actor—he did both gay and straight porn—but also as a prostitute whose "escort" services were advertised on gay site Rentboy.

"I do believe that there should be strict rules for crossover," porn star Shay Fox tells the *Weekly*. "That's where the problem is."

A former porn star who did not want her name used says that many who work in adult video believe "HIV is hard to get." And, she added, "It really is."

The subtext among some straight actors is that it's hard to get—unless you're gay.

At a summer press conference, AHF's Weinstein called criticism of crossover performers "just code" for gay bashing. He told the *Weekly*, "There's a myriad amount of dangers" for all performers "and the reality is you can get tested today and get infected tomorrow."

Indeed, some porn insiders admit that run-of-the-mill STDs are common—so much so that outbreaks are sometimes "covered up with makeup so it doesn't show up on camera," says former performer Gina Rodriguez.

The industry's testing system "is a joke," she says. "Think about it. This is the truth. If I took my test twenty-nine days ago,

I'm okay to work with you because I have a valid test."

The "dirty secret" of porn isn't "crossover," says Weinstein. It's taking escorting jobs, or what some in the business call "making appearances" with fans such as Charlie Sheen. (Sheen seemed to have no problem tracking down some of his favorite adult performers during his famous meltdown last winter.)

"I said fifty percent of the women in porn were 'escorting' back in the late '90s," says adult filmmaker Whiteacre. "The number is certainly higher today."

Escorting is porn without the lights and cameras but definitely with the action. Whether it's safe is a question for its practitioners. Some experts say, ironically or not, condoms usually are required by the individual women themselves for such off-set activity.

"Even if the girls are using condoms when they're escorting, it's doubtful they're going to be kept totally clean," says former performer Rodriguez. "There's a lot of contact there."

Some of the biggest names in the business, such as Charmane Star and Sativa Rose, can easily be found offering private meet-ups—by the hour—on some of L.A.'s classified-ad sites. It's not clear if someone is just capitalizing on the monikers of famous porn stars or if such ads are for real. Neither of those advertisers responded to our email requests for comment.

One porn star, Adora Cash, openly advertises on her own site that she's an "adult film star, escort, domina" and "webcam fetishist."

And a performer who quit the business last year and is now a full-time escort told the *Weekly* that prostitution is so widespread that "most of the female porn stars are escorts."

"Most of all the girls I know that are porn stars I met on set—they all escort, all of them," she adds. "These performers are going out and being irresponsible in their own private sex lives."

★ ★ ★

An uneasy compromise may be the answer. Condoms for anal and vaginal sex are on the table at Cal-OSHA, as officials there draw up the new rule to cover porn. AHF's Weinstein says he won't demand the use of condoms for oral sex. It's a compromise, he says, that is "a reasonable accommodation" for both sides.

And that fine-tuning would save the "money shot" because blow jobs wouldn't violate the OSHA rule under development. "There would not be acceptance of condoms for oral sex," Weinstein acknowledges.

Free Speech Coalition chairman Douglas, a powerful voice in the industry, says, "I'm very much a 'never say never' person. I'm interested in a good-faith effort" toward compromise.

Yet FSC executive director Duke warns, "I don't think the industry will budge" by agreeing to the compromise plan coming before Cal-OSHA.

Larry Flynt and Vivid CEO Steven Hirsch, for example, continue to resist the use of on-set condoms for any reason, and Hirsch threatens to leave Los Angeles if restrictions come to pass. "It's a possibility we will be shooting outside California" if the condom rule passes, Hirsch tells the *Weekly*.

The adult-business news site XBIZ conducted a poll over the summer asking industry movers and shakers if they would leave California should condoms become specifically mandatory: More than 60 percent said yes. "I think that it's very possible that an exodus would happen on some level," says XBIZ managing editor Dan Miller.

Weinstein is among many who think the threat to leave Porn Valley is a bluff. Although porn productions are common in Florida and Nevada, and New Hampshire recognized freedom-of-expression protection for porn in 2008, California is the only state where making adult video is widely protected. "That's true," says adult-industry lawyer Diamond—thanks to a 1988 state supreme court case, *California v. Freeman*, which found that prostitution could be tolerated in cases where pornographic imagery was being produced.

"There's only one state where [porn] is not considered prostitution," says Weinstein—California. "I think if the industry tried to pick up stakes and go, there they would have difficulty. They can't exist as an above-ground industry anywhere else but California."

"They're not going anywhere," agrees porn veteran Margold. "We have been blessed with the Freeman decision."

Attorney Douglas of FSC says the threat to leave is real, though, noting that much production has already gone to Florida, where online juggernaut Manwin has a large presence, and to Nevada, home of the brothel.

"The adult industry is incredibly mobile," he says, "and there's production everywhere. This is a huge amount of money and commerce and employment that would be driven out due to the threat of bad regulation."

A springtime party at R Lounge in Studio City is billed as a chance to meet porn stars, and it is. The high rollers driving up to the red carpet in German cars have to pay a cover charge. The women, of course, get in free. And for the most part you can smell them before they even enter the doors of this modern, minimalist club.

A cloud of marijuana smoke precedes a trio of performers in ten-dollar minidresses and Lucite stripper shoes. They can barely keep their clothes on as a dozen photogs from websites you've never heard of go wild.

One woman flashes her breasts, another turns around and

exposes the back of her thong, and when the performers plop onto a low-slung couch there's no need for that wiggling wardrobe dance familiar to any woman who has worn a short skirt. Panty shots are part of the deal.

The other side of the often dull and technical nature of on-set porn is the "lifestyle" beyond the set. While many female performers view men as "walking wallets," as Margold puts it, they also sometimes genuinely embrace the party and the chance at a side-door entrance to stardom.

Jenna Jameson is perhaps the ultimate porn success, a woman who never did the kind of "gonzo" films that give performers STDs, an entrepreneur who ultimately produced and distributed her own product. Sasha Gray, who quit the industry earlier this year, has crossed over into indie film (*The Girlfriend Experience*) and cable (*Entourage*). The new girls want to be Jenna and Sasha.

Many female porn stars have taken to social media to brag about their cars, their designer handbags, the celebrities they get to meet and the crazy parties they attend. There's plenty of hope among the new talent, even if the jobs are more scarce than they've been in a generation.

Tom Byron, a legendary performer, is thoughtful, honest and reflective when the *Weekly* catches him between takes on the set of *Star Wars XXX*. He's been around the industry long enough— nearly thirty years—to remember the days before testing, which he called "scary."

"Should we probably use condoms?" he asks. "Yes. Do people want to see it? No."

Indeed, the biggest problem for porn is the silent majority: the viewer, the connoisseur, the guy with his thumb on the fast-forward button. Like spectators at a Roman gladiator battle, they want porn to show them the money.

Margold, who has watched the industry progress since Linda Lovelace discovered the fictional clitoris in her throat in 1972, is very much pro condom. In fact, he thinks performers should be tested for intravenous drug use and that new performers should be at least twenty-one.

But, he argues, the consumer's carnal desires are too powerful for even the state of California's workplace police to overcome.

He delivers the money quote, the bottom line:

"We're gotten off to, by society, with its left hand," he says, "and then denied with its right hand. The very people who jack off to us don't give a damn about us, and probably won't."

Lost Boys
Kristen Hinman

Life is life, and you gotta do what you gotta do. It's like everybody can't be a doctor, a teacher, or have rich parents take care of us. And it's gonna teach us, like—when we get older, we're gonna be stronger, 'cause we know life experience and stuff like that. And we're goin' to know what to do in certain situations because of what we've been through when we were younger. You gotta do what you gotta do to survive.

—female, age sixteen

The first night Ric Curtis and Meredith Dank went looking for child prostitutes in the Bronx back in the summer of 2006, they arrived at Hunts Point with the windows of Curtis's decaying Oldsmobile, circa 1992, rolled down. Curtis, who chairs the anthropology department at the John Jay College of Criminal Justice in Manhattan, had done research on the neighborhood's junkies and was well acquainted with its reputation for prostitution (immortalized in several HBO documentaries). If the borough had a centralized stroll for hookers, he figured Hunts Point would be it.

But after spending several hours sweating in the muggy August air, the professor and his PhD student decided to head home. They'd found a grand total of three hookers. Two were underage, and all three were skittish about climbing into a car with two strangers and a tape recorder.

Dispirited though they may have been, the researchers had no intention of throwing in the towel. They were determined to achieve their goal: to conduct a census of New York City's child sex workers.

Even before they'd begun gearing up for the project two months prior, Curtis and Dank knew the magnitude of the challenge they had on their hands. No research team before them had hit on a workable method of quantifying this elusive population. For decades most law-enforcement officials, social workers, and activist groups had cited a vast range—anywhere from tens of thousands to three million—when crafting a sound bite pegging the population of underage hookers nationwide. But the range had been calculated with little or no direct input from the children themselves.

Over time, the dubious numbers became gospel.

In similar fashion, monetary outlays based on the veracity of those numbers began to multiply.

The $500,000 the federal government had allotted for this joint study by John Jay and New York's public-private Center for Court Innovation was chump change compared to the bounty amassed by a burgeoning assortment of nonprofit groups jockeying to liberate and rehabilitate the captive legions of exploited and abused children.

Now Ric Curtis intended to go the direct route in deter-
mining how many kids were out there hooking: he and Dank
were going to locate them, make contact with them, and interview them one-on-one, one kid at a time. If they could round
up and debrief two hundred youths, the research team would
be able to employ a set of statistically solid metrics to accurately
extrapolate the total population.

It took two years of sleuthing, surveying and data-crunching,
but in 2008 Curtis and Dank gave the feds their money's worth—
and then some.

The results of the John Jay survey shattered the widely
accepted stereotype of a child prostitute: a pre- or barely teenage
girl whose every move was dictated by the wiliest of pimps.

After their first attempt flopped, the two researchers switched
tacks. They printed a batch of coupons that could be redeemed
for cash and which listed a toll-free number that kids could call
anonymously to volunteer for the survey. With a local nonprofit
agency that specialized in at-risk youth on board to distribute an
initial set of the coupons, the researchers forwarded the 1-800
line to Dank's cell phone and waited.

It took almost a week, but the line finally lit up. Soon afterward Dank met her first two subjects—one male, the other
female—at a cafe near Union Square. Both were too old to
qualify for the study, and the man said he'd never engaged in sex
for pay. But Dank decided to stay and interview them.

The woman said she had worked as a prostitute and that she
was confident she could send underage kids Dank's way. The
man said he was twenty-three, just out of jail and homeless.

"Out of the two of them, I thought she would have been the

catalyst," Dank says now. "But his was the magic coupon."

Within a day her phone was "blowing up" with calls from kids who'd been referred by the homeless man. Almost as quickly word got around that two professors were holding late-afternoon "office hours" at Stuyvesant Park and would pay half the going rate for oral sex in exchange for a brief interview. Before long the researchers found themselves working long past dark, until they'd covered everyone in line or the rats got too feisty.

Nine months later Dank and Curtis had far surpassed their goal, completing interviews with 249 underage prostitutes. From that data, they were able to put a number on the total population of New York's teen sex workers: 3,946.

Most astonishing to the researchers was the demographic profile teased out by the study. Published by the U.S. Department of Justice in September 2008, Curtis and Dank's findings thoroughly obliterated the long-held core assumptions about underage prostitution:

- ▸ Nearly half of the kids—about 45 percent—were boys.
- ▸ Only 10 percent were involved with a "market facilitator" (e.g., a pimp).
- ▸ About 45 percent got into the "business" through friends.
- ▸ More than 90 percent were U.S.-born (56 percent were New York City natives).
- ▸ On average, they started hooking at age fifteen.
- ▸ Most serviced men—preferably white and wealthy.
- ▸ Most deals were struck on the street.
- ▸ Almost 70 percent of the kids said they'd sought

assistance at a youth-service agency at least once.

‣ Nearly all of the youths—95 percent—said they exchanged sex for money because it was the surest way to support themselves.

‣ In other words, the typical kid who is commercially exploited for sex in New York City is not a tween girl, has not been sold into sexual slavery and is not held captive by a pimp.

‣ Nearly all the boys and girls involved in the city's sex trade are going it alone.

Ric Curtis and Meredith Dank were amazed by what their research had revealed. But they were completely unprepared for the way law-enforcement officials and child-advocacy groups reacted to John Jay's groundbreaking study.

"I remember going to a meeting in Manhattan where they had a lot of prosecutors there whose job was to prosecute pimps," Curtis recalls. "They were sort of complaining about the fact that their offices were very well staffed but their workload was— not very daunting, let's say. They had a couple cases, and at every meeting you go to they'd pull out the cherry-picked case of this pimp they had busted, and they'd tell the same story at every meeting. They too were bothered by the fact that they couldn't find any pimps, any girls.

"So I come along and say, 'I found three hundred kids'— they're all perky—but then I say, 'I'm sorry, but only ten percent had pimps.'

"It was like a fart in church. Because basically I was saying their office was a waste of time and money."

★ ★ ★

Jay Albanese, a criminologist at Virginia Commonwealth University who headed up the Justice Department's research arm for four years, says the findings of the John Jay study are among the most interesting he has seen.

"Whether you are a kid or an adult, the issue becomes: To what extent is this voluntary?" Albanese says. "Because you make more money in this than being a secretary? Or because you really have no choices—like, you're running from abuse or caught up in drugs? The question becomes: If Curtis is correct, what do we do with that ninety percent? Do we ignore it? How hard do we look at how they got into that circumstance? You could make the case that for the ninety percent for whom they couldn't find any pimping going on—well, how does it happen?

"It's a very valid question," Albanese continues. "A policy question: To what extent should the public and the public's money be devoted to these issues, whether it's child prostitution or child pimping?"

The Federal Bureau of Investigation is the only agency that keeps track of how many children the legal system rescues from pimps nationwide. The count, which began in June 2003, now exceeds 1,600 as of April of this year, according to the FBI's Innocence Lost website (fbi.gov/about-us/investigate/vc_majorthefts/cac/innocencelost)—an average of about 200 each year.

Through interviews and analysis of public records, Village Voice Media has found that the federal government spends about $20 million a year on public awareness, victims' services, and police work related to domestic human trafficking, with a considerable focus on combating the pimping of children. An additional $50 million-plus is spent annually on youth homeless shelters, and since 1996 taxpayers have contributed a total of $186 million to fund a separate program that provides street outreach to kids who may be at risk of commercial sexual exploitation.

That's at least $80 million doled out annually for law enforcement and social services that combine to rescue approximately two hundred child prostitutes every year. These agencies might improve upon their $400,000-per-rescued-child average if they joined in the effort to develop a clearer picture of the population they aim to aid. But there's no incentive for them to do so when they stand to rake in even more public money simply by staying the course.

At the behest of advocates who work with pimped girls, along with a scattering of U.S. celebrities who help to publicize the cause, the bipartisan Senate tag team of Oregon's Ron Wyden, a Democrat, and John Cornyn of Texas, a Republican, is pushing for federal legislation that would earmark another $12 million to $15 million a year to fund six shelters reserved exclusively for underage victims of sex trafficking. (In an editorial published this past July, Village Voice Media expressed its support for the initiative, now folded into the pending Trafficking Victims Protection Reauthorization Act.)

Though the language of the bill is gender-neutral, some advocates point to the disproportionate influence wielded by groups who direct their efforts exclusively at pimped girls. They worry that anti-sex-trafficking funding might increasingly ignore boys and transgender youths, not to mention kids of any gender who aren't enslaved by a pimp but sell sex of their own volition. Jennifer Dreher, who heads the anti-trafficking program at Safe Horizon, a New York nonprofit whose Streetwork project has targeted juvenile prostitutes and homeless youths since 1984, says if federal lawmakers took the time to read the John Jay report, they would better grasp the complexity of the issue.

"We have been seeing and talking about this population for so long, but that kind of tug-at-your-heartstrings narrative was the only one focused on," Dreher says, referring to the stereotype of the pimped little girl.

Certainly those girls are out there, Dreher says, and they're in need of help and compassion. But they're only a small segment of the underage population commercially exploited for sex. If you want to eradicate the scourge, argues Dreher, "Then you have to recognize the ninety percent of other types of people that this John Jay College study found."

Ric Curtis couldn't agree more. "All of the advocates are focused on girls," he fumes. "I'm totally outraged by that—I can't tell you how angry I am about that. The most-victimized kids that I met with were the boys, especially the straight boys. I felt so bad for those who have no chance with the advocates." More than three years after publishing his study, the researcher still smarts from the cold shoulder that greeted his work.

"[Initially] there were a lot of people enthusiastic in Washington that we found such a large number," he recounts. "Then they look more closely at my findings. And they see, well, it wasn't three hundred kids under the yoke of some pimp; in fact, it was half boys, and only ten percent of all of the kids were being pimped. And [then] it was a very different reception."

Dank, who now researches human trafficking and commercial sex at the nonpartisan Urban Institute in Washington, DC, is equally baffled at the study's lack of traction outside the halls of the Justice Department.

"We're not denying that [pimped girls] exist," she emphasizes. "But if you were to take all the newspaper, magazine and journal articles that have been written on this, you'd come away saying, 'Oh, my god! Every child-prostitution incident involves a pimp situation!' It's this huge thing. Where really, at the end of the day, yes, that is an issue, but we're at the point where we need to look beyond this one subgroup of the population and look at commercial sexual exploitation of children as a whole."

About a year after the John Jay study commenced, the Justice Department set its sights on Atlanta, awarding a $452,000 grant to Mary Finn, a professor of criminal justice at Georgia State University. Finn's 2007 study had two goals: first, to calculate the population of the metro area's underage sex workers. And second, to evaluate the work of an assemblage of government agencies and nonprofits that had joined forces to combat child prostitution.

The coalition Finn was to assess had formed several years prior with $1 million in Justice Department funding. Heading it up: the Juvenile Justice Fund, a child-advocacy agency allied with the Atlanta Women's Foundation and the Harold and Kayrita Anderson Family Foundation. The trio of nonprofits had commissioned a child-prostitution survey whose alarming findings were destined to be regurgitated nationwide by an unquestioning media—and whose methodology, in turn, would be exposed as entirely bogus and discounted by a veritable who's who of child-prostitution researchers.

To kick off the project, Finn arranged a meeting with representatives of the collaboration and invited Curtis along to help break the ice. It seemed like a good idea: Curtis had accrued a wealth of experience thanks to his one-year head start, and the researchers would ultimately share their findings in a final report. But what was intended as an exercise in diplomacy quickly devolved into a debacle.

The get-together began to unravel when Finn explained that the Justice Department's guidelines required her team to gather its data without regard to gender or motive—in other words, that they would be calculating the prevalence of commercial sex among both boys and girls, and that both trafficking and so-called survival sex were fair game.

At that point, Finn recounts, a Juvenile Justice Fund board member angrily objected, insisting that no child would engage in prostitution by choice. Throughout the debate that ensued, not a single representative from the Atlanta advocates' contingent uttered a syllable of support for Finn's approach. Curtis stepped in, noting that Finn's methodology made sense in light of his preliminary findings.

The group wasn't having any of it.

"The members of the collaborative felt the data couldn't be accurate—that maybe that's the case in New York, but it's certainly not how it is here in Atlanta," Finn recalls. "That's when I sensed that they had far more invested—that there was a reason to be so standoffish, to resist so aggressively or assertively, that I wasn't privy to. What was clear to me was the silence of everyone else: there was some issue of control and power."

To this day, Finn says, she's not sure what was behind the hostile reception. But she does provide some compelling historical context.

Back in the late 1990s, she explains, Atlanta women had galvanized to prevent child prostitution. One juvenile-court judge in particular provided a catalyst when she instituted a screening process in her courtroom that was aimed at identifying kids who were engaging in prostitution.

The only children who were questioned about sex work were girls. Boys were never screened.

"The problem was very narrowly defined from the outset," says Finn. "I'm a feminist scholar," she goes on. "I understand the importance of these advocates—who are predominantly women, predominantly concerned about the plight of girls—wanting to retain that focus on that issue. But as a researcher, knowing that this is labeled as 'child exploitation,' and knowing that there are numbers in other cities showing boys are being victimized, I had to argue that this was maybe a small but significant population we had to look at."

Finn soon found herself facing a dilemma on the research front as well.

When Curtis and Dank put out the call for underage sex workers in New York, they were confident they'd be able to find space in an emergency shelter if they encountered an interview subject who appeared to be in immediate peril. Atlanta, on the other hand, was equipped with no emergency shelters for homeless youths. In the absence of any such backstop, Finn concluded, it would be unethical to go hunting for kids to interview.

So she went with Plan B: interviewing law-enforcement agents and social workers, examining arrest records, and mining a countywide database of child-sexual-abuse cases.

Despite the less-than-satisfactory secondary-source approach, Finn figured she'd have plenty of data to mine. After all, she'd seen breathless media reports of trafficking in Atlanta. "The overall market for sex with kids is booming in many parts of the U.S. In Atlanta—a thriving hotel and convention center with a sophisticated airport and ground transportation network—pimps and other lowlifes have tapped into that market bigtime," blared a 2006 *New York Times* story.

"I walked in thinking: This is going to be a huge priority for any agency that is dealing with at-risk youth. I mean, goodness, this must be at the top of their agenda for training, protocol—all of it."

On the contrary, Finn found that most organizations, whether nonprofit or government-run, were not systematically documenting cases of child prostitution. Apart from thirty-one juvenile arrests police had made over a four-year period, there were virtually no numbers for her to compile.

"It was almost like nobody wants to document their existence," Finn says. "Whether it's because they don't want to label the youth, or they don't want other agencies to know they're aware of them because then the call comes—'Well, what are you doing about it?'—I just don't know. It was very odd. The environment we were seeing in the media just looked so different from the environment we walked into."

In September 2008, just as Finn was preparing a summary of her scant findings, the Juvenile Justice Fund announced an ongoing statewide study based on "scientific probability methods," whose results to date pointed to "a significant number of adolescent girls being commercially sexually exploited in Georgia, likely ranging from 200 to 300 girls, on the streets, over the internet, through escort services, and in major hotels every month from August 2007 to May 2008."

Published in 2010, the final report was nearly as ambiguous, though there were more—and even bigger—numbers. According to the Justice Fund's "scientific research study," underwritten with money from the Anderson Family Foundation, each month in Georgia, 7,200 men pay underage girls for 8,700 sex acts, "with an average of 300 acts a day." The report's authors updated their 2008 stat, increasing their underage-hooker count to four hundred.

The *Atlanta Journal-Constitution* trumpeted the report's findings under the headline "City's shame remains; despite crackdowns, Atlanta is still a hub in selling children for sex."

The *Journal-Constitution* did not, however, inform its readers that the "scientific study" was undertaken not by researchers adhering to rigid academic standards, but by the Schapiro Group, an Atlanta public-relations firm hired by the Justice Fund.

Despite the claims to the contrary, there was nothing remotely "scientific" about the research. In order to gauge the number of men who pay for sex with underage girls, the PR firm observed activity at major hotels and on streets thought to be frequented by sex workers. Staffers also called escort services, posing as customers, to inquire into the possibility of hookups with adolescent girls. And they created online ads featuring photos of young-looking females and inviting prospective customers to call a phone number—a line answered by PR firm "operators" posing as pimps and madams. (For more about the Schapiro Group's dubious methods, see "Weird Science," written by Nick Pinto and published in the March 24 issue of Village Voice Media's newsweeklies, citypages.com/2011-03-23/women-s-funding-network-sex-trafficking-study-is-junk-science.)

Mary Finn is troubled by the murky provenance of the statistics, but more so by the time and effort wasted on sensationalizing a problem instead of addressing it.

"This shouldn't be a race to the top," she contends. "We should be mobilized for a single victimization. Why do we need three hundred, or five hundred, or one thousand to mobilize as a community?

"I guess that's what is most disheartening about the [dubious] numerical information that's coming out: we may not be putting resources where we need to put them, because we don't have a clear grasp of what the underlying problem is."

Anyone curious about the underlying problem in New York City can find numerous clues within the 122-page report documenting the several hundred in-person interviews at the core of the John Jay College study.

There are, for instance, the state-run group homes for orphans and kids whose families have kicked them out:

"...[H]e was like, you know, the little leeches that linger around," said a girl who told of being picked up by a pimp outside the group home where she resided at age fifteen. "And I was sittin' on my steps and I was cryin' because they're givin' you allowance—twenty-sumpin' dollars a week—and then you're not allowed to do certain types a jobs because you have a curfew. And if you miss curfew, they shippin' you somewhere else. So it was like, I was just at my rope's end. And the things that he was sayin' to me, it sounded good."

And the potential pitfalls of the foster-care system:

"My mother died and I was placed in foster homes," said a girl who started hooking at age fifteen. "My foster father would touch me, and I ran away. I ended up coming to New York, and I was on the streets; nobody wanted to help me. And I ran into this girl, and she was like thirty-eight when she passed away last year, but she taught me everything I know. She taught me how to do what I have to do—but not be stupid about it—to play it right, and be smart."

Not to mention youth homeless shelters:

"I've been raped at Covenant House three times," one young man stated. "It was by guys in the men's ward." (The three other youths interviewed for the study who spoke specifically about the New York–based nonprofit, whose mission is to care for kids in crisis, made no mention of sexual assault; they described the shelter as a place where kids shared knowledge about how to sell sex and/or characterized it as a popular place for pimps looking to recruit.)

★ ★ ★

One recurring theme is economic desperation:

"The fact that people think that I'm doing it because I want to—I mean, I get replies all the time on email, and they tell me, 'You know, why don't you just get a job?'" reported a boy with three years' experience selling sex. "Well no shit, Sherlock! Honestly! I don't know, I would like someone to be able to offer me something."

Law-enforcement personnel, the kids say, are not always helpful:

"One cop said, 'You're lucky I'm off duty, but you're gonna suck my dick or I'ma take you in,'" a transgender youth stated. "This has happened to me about eight times."

"Police raped me a couple a times in Queens," said a female who had worked as a prostitute for four years. "The last time that happened was a coupla months ago. But you don't tell anybody; you just deal wit' it."

Though many kids said they developed buddy-system strategies to stay safe and fed on the street, nearly all wanted a way out:

"I really wanna stop now, but I can't 'cause I have no source of income since I'm too young," said a girl who'd begun hooking at age twelve. "So it's like that I have to do it, it's not like I wanna do it. As I say, I'm only seventeen, I got a two-year-old daughter, so that means I got pregnant real young. Didn't have no type of Medicaid…. Can't get a job, have no legal guardian, I don't have nobody to help me but [friends], so you know, we all in this together."

In late 2009 the U.S. Department of Justice called on the Center for Court Innovation and John Jay professor Ric Curtis to expand their research to other cities nationwide, backing the project with a $1.275 million federal grant. Now Curtis and Jennifer Bryan, the center's principal research associate, direct six research teams across the United States, employing the same in-the-trenches approach that worked in New York City: respondent-driven sampling, or RDS.

The method was developed in the 1990s by sociologist Doug Heckathorn, now on the faculty at Cornell University, who was seeking a way to count hidden populations. It has since been used in fifteen countries to put a number on a variety of subcultures, from drug addicts to jazz musicians. Curtis and his research assistant, Meredith Dank, were the first to use RDS to count child prostitutes.

For the John Jay study, Curtis and Dank screened kids for two criteria: age (eightgeen and under) and involvement in prostitution. All subjects who completed the study's full, confidential interview were paid twenty dollars. They were also given a stack of coded coupons to distribute to other potential subjects, and for each successful referral they were paid ten dollars. And so on.

RDS relies on a snowball effect that ultimately extends through numerous social networks, broadening the reach of the study. "The benefit of this is that you're getting the hidden population: kids who don't necessarily show up for [social] services and who may or may not get arrested," says Bryan. "It's based on the 'six degrees of separation' theory."

To calculate their population estimate, the John Jay team first culled the interview subjects who didn't fit the study's criteria but had been included for the potential referrals they could generate. The next step was to tally the number of times the remaining 249 subjects had been arrested for prostitution and compare that to the total number of juvenile prostitution arrests in state law-enforcement records. Using a mathematical algorithm often employed in biological and social-science studies, Ric Curtis and his crew were able to estimate that 3,946 youths were hooking in New York.

David Finkelhor, director of the Crimes Against Children Research Center at the University of New Hampshire, calls the New York study significant, in that it "makes the big [national] numbers that people put out—like a million kids, or five hundred thousand kids—unlikely."

Finkelhor's single caveat: while RDS is efficient in circulating through a broad range of social networks, certain scenarios might elude detection—specifically, foreign children who might be held captive and forbidden to socialize.

Still, says Finkelhor, "I think [the study] highlights important components of the problem that don't get as much attention: that there are males involved, and that there are a considerable number of kids who are operating without pimps."

The John Jay study's authors say they were surprised from the start at the number of boys who came forward. In response Dank pursued new avenues of inquiry—visiting courthouses to interview girls who'd been arrested, and canvassing at night with a group whose specialty was street outreach to pimped girls. She and Curtis also pressed their male subjects for leads.

"It turns out that the boys were the more effective recruiter of pimped girls than anybody else," Curtis says. "It's interesting, because this myth that the pimps have such tight control over the girls, that no one can talk to them, is destroyed by the fact that these boys can talk to them and recruit them and bring them to us. Obviously the pimps couldn't have that much of a stranglehold on them."

The same, of course, might be true of the elusive foreign-born contingent Finkelhor mentions.

Curtis and Dank believe there is indeed a foreign sub-population RDS could not reach. But with no data to draw on, it's impossible to gauge whether it's statistically significant or yet another overblown stereotype.

And as the researchers point out, the John Jay study demolished virtually every other stereotype surrounding the underage sex trade.

For the national study, researchers are now hunting for underage hookers in Las Vegas, Dallas, Miami, Chicago and the San Francisco Bay Area, and interviews for an Atlantic City survey are complete.

Curtis is reluctant to divulge any findings while so much work remains to be done, but he does say early returns suggest that the scarcity of pimps revealed by the New York study appears not to be an anomaly.

A final report on the current research is scheduled for completion in mid-2012.

"I think that the study has a chance to dispel some of the myths and a lot of the raw emotion that is out there," says Marcus Martin, the PhD who's leading the Dallas research crew. "At the end of the day, I think the study is going to help the kids, as well as tell their story."

If the work Ric Curtis and Meredith Dank began in New York is indeed going to help the kids, it will do so because it tells their story. And because it addresses the most difficult—and probably the most important—question of all: what drives young kids into the sex trade?

Dallas Police Department Sergeant Byron Fassett, whose police work with underage female prostitutes is hailed by child advocates and government officials including Senator Wyden, believes hooking is "a symptom of another problem that can take many forms. It can be poverty, sexual abuse, mental abuse—there's a whole range of things you can find in there.

"Generally we find physical and sexual abuse or drug abuse when the child was young," Fassett continues. "These children are traumatized. People who are involved in this are trauma-stricken. They've had something happen to them. The slang would be that they were 'broken.'"

Fassett has drawn attention because of his targeted approach to rescuing (rather than arresting) prostitutes and helping them gain access to social services. The sergeant says that because the root causes of youth prostitution can be so daunting to address from a social-policy standpoint, it's easy—and politically expedient—to sweep them under the proverbial rug.

And then there are the John Jay researchers' groundbreaking findings. Though the study could not possibly produce thorough psychological evaluations and case histories, subjects were asked the question: "How did you get into this?" Their candid answers revealed a range of motives and means:

▶ "I can't get a job that would pay better than this."
▶ "I like the freedom this lifestyle affords me."
▶ "My friend was making a lot of money doing it and introduced me to it."
▶ "I want money to buy a new cell phone."

Though the context is a different one, Dank and Curtis have, not unlike Byron Fassett, come to learn that their survey subjects' responses carry implications that are both daunting to address and tempting to deny or ignore.

For example, the John Jay study found that when asked what

it would take to get them to give up prostitution, many kids expressed a desire for stable, long-term housing. But the widely accepted current social-service model—shelters that accommodate, at most, a ninety-day stay—doesn't give youths enough time to get on their feet and instead pushes them back to the streets. The findings also point to a general need for more emphasis on targeted outreach, perhaps through peer-to-peer networks, as well as services of all kinds, from job training and placement to psychological therapy.

Regarding that last area of treatment, Curtis believes that kids who have made their own conscious decision to prostitute themselves might need more long-term help than those who are forced into the trade by someone else.

"Imagine if you take a kid off the street and put them in therapy," he says. "Which do you think is easier to deal with: the kid who's been enslaved by another human being, or the one who's been enslaved by him- or herself—who only have themselves to blame? In my view, healing those kids is a steeper hill than the one who can point to somebody and say, 'He did that to me, I'm not that kind of person,' and who can deflect the blame."

Which raises the question: who's willing to pay the freight to guide kids up that hill?

The Original Blonde
Neal Gabler

Jean Harlow, who would have celebrated her one hundredth birthday this year, was so original a sex goddess that she invented a whole new style in cinematic seduction. When Harlow burst onto the Hollywood scene in the early 1930s, there had been vamps and sirens and floozies and hussies and slatterns and It girls and nice girls next door. But there had never been a bombshell. As the word implies, being a bombshell meant that you detonated. Harlow was certainly that kind of ordnance. She didn't just appear on-screen, she exploded. Novelist Graham Greene wrote, "She toted a breast like a man totes a gun." She was brassy, sassy, no-nonsense, tough, self-possessed, carefree, wildly extroverted and, of course, buxom. Her hair was the color of platinum, her skin the color of alabaster. Though she was a tiny woman, there was always something outsize about her, a sexual too-muchness that made her the perfect antidote to the parsimony of the Great

Depression. Other actresses frowned. Harlow always wore a giant smile to signal just how much fun she was having. Inevitably, Harlow's style became a national style. Women peroxided their hair and painted their lips in a Cupid's bow the way Harlow did so they could not only look like Harlow but attempt to *be* like Harlow. She was a force untamed.

What made Harlow original wasn't the type of dame she played. Marlene Dietrich once described her as a "tart with a heart," and her basic persona was the familiar one of a cynical, hardboiled broad on the outside hiding a sentimental, decent girl on the inside. Her originality was in her attitude—in the way she flaunted herself as her own aesthetic object. Her characters are not only outré, they cultivate that quality. They luxuriate in it. They are highly conscious of the effect it has, especially on men. In some ways it makes Harlow the first postmodernist sex symbol. One part of her, the mental part, was always measuring the other part of her, the physical part. No sex symbol has ever been as brainily self-aware.

That physicality was also like no other actress's before her. If Harlow on-screen seemed to be loose figuratively, a good-time girl who threw herself at men, she was also loose literally. Where her major screen rivals, Greta Garbo, Joan Crawford, Norma Shearer and Bette Davis, were all thin, hard, bony and aristocratic, Harlow was soft and uncorseted—the kind of woman a man wanted to squeeze and bury himself in. Her softness was accentuated by the silky gowns she often wore draped lightly over her luscious body so you could see the contours underneath. This wasn't sex by suggestion; this was the real thing. The fact that Harlow never wore a brassiere was almost as much a trademark as her hair. When she moved, she jiggled—not just her ample breasts but her whole being. It was as if, in freeing herself from her undergarments, she had also freed herself from the restraints of her age.

Harlow's flouncy freedom made a lasting impression, one of the most iconic of Hollywood, and it is all the more remarkable when we consider how young she was and how short her career was. She was born Harlean Carpenter in Kansas City, Missouri, to an erstwhile-dentist father and an overbearing, social-climbing mother whose family had come into wealth through real estate. The mother, named Jean, had acting aspirations herself. She divorced the dentist and took her daughter to Hollywood. When her career didn't pan out, she slunk back East. It was that summer, while dining at the Sherman House hotel in Chicago between trains, after Jean had picked Harlean up from camp, that they met an ambitious con man named Marino Bello, who was so smitten with Mama Jean that he got a divorce and married her. Meanwhile, Jean enrolled Harlean in boarding school in Lake Forest, Illinois, where a classmate introduced her to a young man whose parents had died in a boating accident, leaving him their fortune. The two decided to elope. Harlean was only sixteen. Both couples then headed back to California.

Despite the fact that she was already fetching, Harlean had no Hollywood ambitions. She was happy to be a teenage housewife. But as the story goes, she was hosting a luncheon for some friends when one of them said she had to leave for an appointment with a casting director at Fox Studios. Harlean offered to drive her, and naturally she caught the casting director's eye. He gave her a letter of introduction to the Central Casting Bureau, which hired extras. Harlean filed it away until another friend dared her to go. She took the dare, signing the register as "Jean Harlow," her mother's maiden name, and thus began her film career.

It wasn't much of a career at first. She was just an extra, but she was a noticeable extra. Eventually producer Hal Roach signed her to a five-year contract, mainly playing eye candy in two-reel comedies. While working as an extra in a ballroom scene in a feature comedy, she came to the attention of actor James Hall. Hall invited her to shoot a screen test for his next picture, a World War I epic titled *Hell's Angels* that young millionaire Howard Hughes was producing and directing. Hughes had begun the film as a silent with Norwegian actress Greta Nissen in the female lead, but when he decided to convert it to a talkie, he needed an English-speaking actress to replace her. Hence Harlow's screen test. Hughes gave her the part and a contract.

You could say the rest is history, except it wasn't. Harlow got brutal reviews playing the trampy girlfriend of a British flier in the picture. And though she was certainly an eye magnet, critics ridiculed her acting abilities in movie after movie, even as her roles grew. "It is unfortunate that Jean Harlow, whose virtues as an actress are limited to her blonde beauty, has to carry a good share of the picture," said one critic of her performance in *Iron Man*. "The acting throughout is interesting, with the exception of Jean Harlow," opined the *New York Times* critic of her performance in *The Public Enemy*. "Miss Harlow, as the society girl, is competent but not much more," wrote another critic of her performance in *Platinum Blonde*. This was the consensus. Perhaps no other major star had been flagellated by the critics as much as and for as long as Harlow was. It was almost as if they resented her man-taunting routine—or at least the obviousness of it. That may have been because Harlow hadn't evolved into Harlow yet. She hadn't learned how to make that routine her own.

The tide began to turn when MGM, the biggest and most glamorous of studios, purchased her contract from Hughes and cast her as a wanton working girl who seduces her rich boss into marrying her in *Red-Headed Woman,* made under the supervision of production wunderkind Irving Thalberg. Part of the critical reversal may have been the change in hair color so that Harlow couldn't be accused of acting with her perm. But a larger part of it was almost certainly the abandon with which she approached the role—the scale of her performance. Harlow finally gave a performance large enough to match the extremes of her sexy appearance. She wasn't acting to type as she had in her earlier pictures; she was creating a new type: a woman with a liberating lust and appetite and a certain degree of calculation about how to use them. She was a happy conniver.

The tide turned further when MGM paired her with one of its biggest male stars, Clark Gable, in *Red Dust.* The two had appeared together in a crime melodrama, *The Secret Six,* when both were bit players, but stardom liberated them, made them bigger, matching Gable's hyperbolic male with Harlow's hyperbolic female. Their screen romance is based not on great professions of love or treacly sentiments but on mutual toughness, on a *lack* of conventional romance. They are both hard-bitten cynics, people who have been around the block and know the score, and their relationship is a battle of wills that in some ways helped reinvent the whole idea of love. For them, love isn't lofty. It is both primal and practical—a deal.

These MGM pictures softened the critical whippings Harlow had received, but what catapulted her into the first rank of stars was a discovery she made early on, one that the studios were slow to recognize. Harlow knew she wasn't a great dramatic actress. She realized as well that playing gun molls, tramps and hookers was a dead end. More to the point, she understood how ridiculous the exaggerated sexuality she projected was—from the hair to the makeup to the gowns to the lipstick. She realized that the lusty, wisecracking girl she typically played wasn't a tragic figure but a comic one and that she herself was basically a comedienne who appreciated just how much fun (and how funny) sex could be. As *Time* wrote in 1934, "Instead of becoming Hollywood's number one siren, she has become its number one comedienne." In truth, she was both.

Mae West had already made the same discovery about sex and humor, turning herself into a parody of the man-eating woman. The difference between West and Harlow was not only one of degree—Harlow was soft and accessible, while West was like a fortress—but also one of self-consciousness. West was a joke, and her movies were basically occasions for her to make wry, suggestive comments, mutter innuendos and issue ripostes. They are cold because West shows us only one side of herself. Harlow was less a joke than she was jokey. Her movies, though not necessarily any funnier than West's, are more human and even occasionally touching because Harlow had that self-regard—that postmodernist ability to stand back and view her own image—that West didn't have. West was all one thing: a sexual omnivore. Harlow was several things at once, not least a body and a brain.

Harlow wasn't just a simple floozy. As she moved more deeply into comedy, contradictions emerged in her screen persona, many of them having sprung from her own life. She was both a sophisticate and an innocent, both cagey and obtuse, both hardboiled and tenderhearted. All these qualities no doubt contributed to her appeal, since they gave her a breadth few previous sex symbols had. But the biggest of these contradictions may have been the one between woman and child. For all intents and purposes, Harlow was a child. She was still in her early twenties when she began to achieve stardom, and in some ways she was even younger than her years. Her mother had called her Baby from birth and continued to use the nickname even as Harlow ascended Hollywood's ranks (in fact, everyone in Hollywood called her the Baby). She also treated Harlow as if she were a baby, forcing Harlow to live with her and managing her business affairs along with Bello, a sharpie who never saw an angle he didn't want to exploit.

The great irony of America's greatest sex symbol of the time is that she might have preferred her mother's company to that of her husbands and lovers. Mama wrecked Harlow's first marriage to the young heir with whom she had eloped as a teenager, forcing her to get an abortion for fear that a baby would ruin her career. She later forced her daughter to get a divorce. Mama disapproved of Harlow's second marriage, to MGM producer Paul Bern, a man twenty-one years Harlow's senior. When Bern died of a gunshot wound—either suicide or murder—Harlow returned to Mama. Mama effectively destroyed Harlow's third marriage too, to cinematographer Harold Rosson, even demanding that he sign a postnuptial agreement. Observing the family dynamic when Mama and her husband visited the set as he directed Harlow in *Platinum Blonde,* Frank Capra said, "I could tell the whole story right there. She was dominated. She wanted her mother, she loved her mother and she wanted to be near her mother." In short, Harlow had a lot of men, but no man could have her. She belonged to Mama alone.

This wasn't just a personal peculiarity. Harlow managed to incorporate her infantilism into her work. On-screen as well as off, she was a beautiful, vivacious, randy woman—but also an emotional child prone to demands, outbursts and tantrums. Her characters kept oscillating between the two. Similarly, her on-screen lovers seemed to be torn between wanting to bed her and wanting to take care of her. That way Harlow covered both bases. And in doing so, just as she led the way in creating the bombshell and the unromantic romance, she led the way in creating the child-woman too. Marilyn Monroe (who so admired Harlow that she got Harlow's hairdresser to dye her locks platinum), Jayne Mansfield, Barbara Nichols, Goldie Hawn and scores of other blondes owed a debt to Harlow as they played the child-woman bit, though most of them did so less tempestuously than Harlow did.

But it was a tough image to maintain, this larger-than-life sexual predator who was also something of a babe, and Harlow herself was ambivalent about it. There were times she seemed to encourage the conflation of woman and persona. Like her characters, she had numerous affairs and not always with the most savory of men. Among her conquests was the notorious gangster Abner "Longy" Zwillman, whom, according to one account, she had met alongside Al Capone. She also bedded director Howard Hawks, writer Thomas Wolfe and boxer Max Baer. Her best and most diligent biographer, David Stenn, says that she suffered from venereal disease, and another biographer claims that she gaily revealed her vagina to reporters to show that her pubic hair had also been dyed platinum, and that once, in despair, she walked the streets, trying to pick up men. She also liked to cozy up with a bottle of Graves gin. And beyond the romances, the alleged promiscuity and the boozing, the mysterious death of her second husband, Paul Bern, dragged her into scandal and real-life melodrama and made her seem more like her screen persona.

By the same token, she often lamented that she was constantly being confused for the characters she played and practically begged the studio to give her a role as a good girl for once—a role, as she put it, "in which I wouldn't have to speak bad English and slink up to 'my man.'" She complained that she spent so much time developing her characters on-screen that she never had time to develop herself. "If I could put on the Harlow personality like a mask while I was working and take it off when the day was done," she said, "that would be heaven. I can't ever be myself." In reality Harlow was well-read and well-spoken and had even written a novel. This was the intellectual Harlow—the brainy screen superego who regarded and sometimes manipulated the Harlow id. All too often, though, the superego seemed to be subordinated to that id.

Harlow wasn't the only one protesting her image. The forces of censorship were none too happy with the loose, liberated, sexy, uninhibited Harlow. In 1934, when they successfully pressured the studios to enforce a production code that legislated screen behavior, Harlow was a primary target. She complied—gladly, she said. Part of the makeover was getting rid of her platinum hair. "I've always hated my hair," she proclaimed, "not only because it limited me as an actress but because it limited me as a person." Another time she said, "I'm tired of playing second to a head of hair," and the platinum blonde became a "brownette." She was less flouncy too, her great uncorseted wardrobe replaced by dresses that covered more than they exposed. If she had begun her career tumbling out of the era, she was now being held in. It was more than a professional strategy to appease the censors; it seemed to be a way for Harlow to get back to herself—to rediscover the woman she believed was hidden under the old image.

But try as she might to change it, that image continued to haunt her. It haunted her when she began a long romance with the suave star William Powell, who had recently been divorced from another sexy comedienne, Carole Lombard. Harlow confessed she loved Powell, and he, for his part, kept squiring her, but he also refused to marry her, because, he said, Hollywood marriages didn't work. He had Harlow's own record to prove it. Brownette hair and cotton dresses notwithstanding, the bombshell couldn't domesticate herself enough for Powell.

But the image had an even more dire consequence. In the end she may have died because of the expectations with which it burdened her. It was clear while she was making *Saratoga* with Clark Gable that she was feeling fatigued and out of sorts. She even collapsed on the set. One suspects that had this been fragile Greta Garbo, the studio would have hospitalized her immediately and halted production on the film. But this was Harlow—young, bouncy, bawdy, wild, hard-bitten Jean Harlow. It was difficult to imagine Harlow being out of commission for long. She was too much of a life force for anything to repress her. But that wasn't the only reason she didn't get the proper ministrations. By one account, her personal doctor refused to tend to her because his wife was afraid he might succumb to Harlow's temptations. Instead he sent an older colleague, who misdiagnosed Harlow's condition and hydrated her when he should have been administering diuretics. Harlow was in renal failure, possibly the long-delayed result of damage to her kidneys during a bout of scarlet fever in 1925 that was followed by a severe infection. By the time she was transferred to Good Samaritan Hospital, the prognosis was hopeless. She died the morning of June 7, 1937. She was just twenty-six years old.

It was a short life and a short career with some fabulous movies. Those are clearly her legacies, but she left another legacy too, a cultural one. It was in how she helped shape romance and sexuality for generations to come. In inventing the blonde bombshell, Harlow practically invented the idea that sexuality could be big, tough, daring and as outlandishly obvious as her whitish hair and slinky gowns. And that it could be very, very funny if you didn't take it too seriously. Harlow's bequest, then, is not just a glamorous look but a whole sexual sensibility of ticklish joy that is so natural to us now that we assume it must have been that way all along. But it began with Jean Harlow.

About the Authors

INSIYA ANSARI is a writer with roots in the San Francisco Bay Area.

ROB BOSTON is senior policy analyst for Americans United for Separation of Church and State in Washington, DC. He also serves as assistant editor of AU's monthly magazine *Church & State*. Boston joined the Americans United staff in 1987 and is the author of three books on church–state relations.

PATRICK CALIFIA (née Pat Califia, prior to a gender transition from female to male) has been writing about sex practically since this activity was invented. SRSLY. He is the author of a dozen or so nonfiction and fiction books that explore the issue of sexual variation, the parameters of gender, and confronting the repression and social control of pleasure.

SETH FISCHER's writing has appeared on The Rumpus, Pank, Guernica, Monkeybicycle, Gertrude and elsewhere. He also teaches at Antioch University Los Angeles and Writing Workshops Los Angeles. His in-progress essay collection is called *How To Grow Up Gracefully.*

NEAL GABLER is an author, scholar and teacher. He has won two *Los Angeles Times* Book Prizes (for *An Empire of Their Own* and *Walt Disney: The Triumph of the American Imagination),* and his biography of Walter Winchell, *Winchell: Gossip, Power and the Culture of Celebrity,* was named the book of the year by *Time* Magazine.

NICHOLAS GARNETT (nicholasgarnett.com) received his MFA in creative writing from Florida International University (FIU). He teaches creative writing at FIU, the Center for Literature and Theatre at Miami Dade College, and is the nonfiction editor of the literary journal *Sliver of Stone.* He lives and writes in Miami Beach, Florida.

MELISSA GIRA GRANT (postwhoreamerica.com) is an independent journalist and blogger. She's written for AlterNet, Wired. com, Slate, *The Guardian, Glamour,* the *New York Observer*'s Betabeat, Truthout, TheNation.com, Jezebel, and the award-winning *$pread* magazine, among others. Her work has previously appeared in *Best Sex Writing.*

CONNER HABIB is an essay and fiction writer, a porn star and a lecturer who lives in San Francisco. He also runs a Rudolf Steiner discussion group, writes plays, is NewNowNext's sex expert and is working on a podcast featuring leading thinkers at the intersections of science, spirituality and culture. His blog is connerhabib.wordpress.com and his twitter is @ConnerHabib.

KRISTEN HINMAN covered crime, politics, education and many other subjects for Village Voice Media from 2004 to 2011. She edits political coverage for *Bloomberg Businessweek* magazine.

ANDY ISAACSON (andyisaacson.net) is a freelance writer and photographer. His work has appeared in *The New York Times, The Atlantic, Wired* and NewYorker.com.

JONATHAN ALLEN LETHEM (born February 19, 1964) is an American novelist, essayist and short story writer. His first novel, *Gun, with Occasional Music*, was published in 1994. In 1999, Lethem published *Motherless Brooklyn*, a National Book Critics Circle Award–winning novel that achieved mainstream success. In 2003, he published *The Fortress of Solitude*, which became a *New York Times* Best Seller. In 2005, he received a MacArthur Fellowship.

ALEX MORRIS is a Contributing Editor at *New York* magazine. She has also written for *Rolling Stone, Glamour* and *Details*, among others. She lives in Brooklyn, New York.

JON PRESSICK is a sex writer, editor, organizer and gadabout. He contributes to Met Another Frog (mctanotherfrog.com), and edited their recent book *Asses to Asses, Bust to Bust*. He is focusing on his blog Sex In Words (sex-in-words.blogspot.ca), writing erotica and curating the Toronto Erotica Writers and Readers Group.

DENNIS ROMERO has been writing about pop culture for twenty years, covering everything from surfing to the porn industry, electronic dance music to Los Angeles gang culture. He's been on staff at the *Los Angeles Times,* the *Philadelphia Inquirer, Ciudad* magazine and *LA Weekly,* where he writes news.

LORI SELKE lives in Oakland, California. She has been writing about sex for nearly twenty years and her work has appeared in *Everything You Know About Sex is Wrong* as well as at SexIs.com and the Good Vibrations Magazine "Sexy Mama" blog. Her collection of (mostly) dyke sex stories, *Lost Girls and Others,* is available from Renaissance eBooks.

JULIA SERANO (*juliaserano.com)* is a writer, performer, and author of *Whipping Girl: A Transsexual Woman on Sexism and the Scapegoating of Femininity* (Seal Press, 2007). Her writings have appeared in numerous anthologies and magazines, and have been used as teaching materials in gender and sexuality studies courses across North America.

RACHEL SWAN was a staff writer at the *East Bay Express.* She is a reformed Luddite and an incorrigible flirt.

MADISON YOUNG's work includes documenting our sexual culture in her feminist erotic films and serving as the Artistic Director of the forward-thinking nonprofit arts organization, Femina Potens Art Gallery. Her writings have been published in *The Ultimate Guide to Kink; Baby Remember My Name; Rope, Bondage, and Power* and *In Soumises.* Her memoir "Daddy" will be available in fall 2013 through Barnacle Books Publishing.

About the Editors

RACHEL KRAMER BUSSEL (rachelkramerbussel.com) is a New York–based author, editor and blogger. She has edited over forty books of erotica, including *Anything for You; Suite Encounters; Going Down; Irresistible; Gotta Have It; Obsessed; Women in Lust; Surrender; Orgasmic; Cheeky Spanking Stories; Bottoms Up; Spanked: Red-Cheeked Erotica; Fast Girls; Smooth; Passion; The Mile High Club; Do Not Disturb; Going Down; Tasting Him; Tasting Her; Please, Sir; Please, Ma'am; He's on Top; She's on Top; Caught Looking; Hide and Seek; Crossdressing; Rubber Sex,* and is *Best Sex Writing* series editor. Her anthologies have won 8 IPPY (Independent Publisher) Awards, and *Surrender* won the National Leather Association Samois Anthology Award. Her work has been published in over one hundred anthologies, including *Best American Erotica 2004* and *2006*. She wrote the popular "Lusty Lady" column for the *Village Voice*.

Rachel has written for *AVN, Bust,* Cleansheets.com, *Cosmopolitan, Curve,* The Daily Beast, TheFrisky.com, *Glamour,* Gothamist, Huffington Post, *Inked,* Mediabistro, *Newsday, New York Post, New York Observer, Penthouse,* The Root, Salon, *San Francisco Chronicle, Time Out New York* and *Zink,* among others. She has appeared on "The Gayle King Show," "The Martha Stewart Show," "The Berman and Berman Show," NY1 and Showtime's "Family Business." She hosted the popular In the Flesh Erotic Reading Series (inthefleshreadingseries.com), featuring readers from Susie Bright to Zane, and speaks at conferences, does readings and teaches erotic writing workshops across the country. She blogs at lustylady.blogspot.com.

CAROL QUEEN (carolqueen.com) has a PhD in sexology and a prior degree in sociology. She calls herself a *cultural sexologist;* while she addresses individual and couple's sexual concerns, her overarching interest is in cultural issues (gender, shame, access to education, et cetera.). She is the author or editor of a dozen books, including Lambda Literary Award winner, *PoMoSexuals* (edited with Lawrence Schimel), *Exhibitionism for the Shy* and *Real Live Nude Girl: Chronicles of Sex-Positive Culture.* She is the cofounder and executive director of The Center for Sex & Culture, a nonprofit sex ed/arts center in San Francisco (sexandculture.org), is Staff Sexologist at Good Vibrations (goodvibes.com), and frequently speaks at colleges and universities about sexuality. She blogs at the Good Vibes Magazine and contributes to the Boston Dig. She lives in San Francisco with Robert, Dina, Teacup and Bracelet, two of whom are cats.

Grateful acknowledgment is made for permission to reprint the following essays: "Live Nude Models" by Jonathan Lethem was published in *Playboy*, August 2011 issue. "Can a Better Vibrator Inspire an Age of Great American Sex?" by Andy Isaacson was published in The Atlantic.com, May 14, 2012. "Sex by Numbers" by Rachel Swan was published in *East Bay Express*, November 30, 2011. "Very Legal: Sex and Love in Retirement" by Alex Morris was published in *New York* magazine, August 6, 2012 issue. "Notes from a Unicorn" by Seth Fischer was published February 24, 2012 at TheRumpus.net. "Rest Stop Confidential" by Conner Habib was published March 28, 2012 on Salon.com. "When on Fire Island... A Polyamorous Disaster" by Nicholas Garnett was published as "Our Polyamory Disaster" January 19, 2012 on Salon.com. "Cherry Picking" by Julia Serano was published in *Trans/Love: Radical Sex, Love & Relationships Beyond the Gender Binary* edited by Morty Diamond (Manic D Press, 2011). "Baby Talk" by Rachel Kramer Bussel was published May 7, 2012 on Salon.com. "Sex by Any Other Name" by Insiya Ansari was published in *Love, InshAllah: The Secret Love Lives of American Muslim Women* edited by Ayesha Mattu and Nura Maznavi (Soft Skull Press, 2012). "Submissive: A Personal Manifesto" by Madison Young and "Enhancing Masochism" by Patrick Califia were published in *The Ultimate Guide to Kink: BDSM, Role Play and The Erotic Edge* by Tristan Taormino (Cleis Press, 2012). "Happy Hookers" by Melissa Gira Grant was published in Jacobin (http://jacobinmag.com/), Summer 2012 issue. "Christian Conservatives vs. Sex: The Long War Over Reproductive Freedom" by Rob Boston was published in *Church & State Magazine* (May, 2012). "Porn Defends the Money Shot" by Dennis Romero was published in *LA Weekly*, September 29, 2011. "Lost Boys" by Kristin Hinman was published in *Riverfront Times*, November 2, 2011. "The Original Blonde" by Neil Gabler was published in *Playboy*, December 2011 issue.